Pizza Memoirs

Desert View Publishing

First Edition: September 2012

Printed in the United States of America

ISBN 978-0-615-63780-8

Pizza Memoirs

Linda S. Groves

For my family,
whose love is my greatest blessing

Thank You

I am so grateful to my daughter Jen Groves and my sister Elaine Jones. Were it not for their disagreement over what I should serve for dinner one night, this book may never have been written. Elaine wanted pizza and Jen wanted a fresh salad so, in my effort to avoid conflict, I turned Jen's favorite traditional Caprese salad into a dynamite artisanal pizza. After a few bites, Elaine looked across the table and said, "You know, you should write a pizza cookbook." The rest, as they say, is history!

A special thank you to my friend Judi Oderkirk who listened as I searched for words that would capture the true essence of this book, what it represented to me, and what I wanted it to be for my readers. She suggested the perfect title – **Pizza Memoirs**.

Thank you to my family, friends and hospice patients for sharing your food memories with me; your stories inspired me and it is all of you whom I honor with the recipes in this book.

To our out of state guests, Matt, Kim, and Julia Groves, Jennifer Groves, Elaine and Ervin Jones, Mark, Eli and Margaux Rajotte who ate nothing but pizza on their visits so I could get all the recipes tested, I am most grateful to you for your willingness to push beyond the boundaries of normal taste-testing and 'take one for the team.' Our friends Gary and Judi Oderkirk taste-tested pizzas weekly before moving to Washington and I thank them for being so encouraging in the early days when some ingredients just did not work together and I occasionally incinerated a crust on their grill.

I am indebted to all those who attended taste-testing sessions over the years – Araceli Martinez, Gloria Fisch, Julie Johnson, Judy Volpe, Patty Price, Sue Manthey, Gwen Jurgens, and John and Barbara Merlin. Barbara tested some recipes on her own, as did Bryan Seifert and his wife, Sonia in Chicago...*mil gracias* – a thousand thanks. A special thank you goes to Charlie and Faith Bull, our neighbors and good friends who have been in the thick of pizza testing for the past few years. They would graciously stop what they were doing whenever my husband Charlie ran across the street with a few pieces of pizza for them to try; they would taste it and report back within minutes – good, bad or indifferent.

Also I thank Kevin Jones and Anthony DeConcini, the talented and creative design team at AlphaGraphics with whom I had the pleasure to work.

And then there's the tedious, technical part of the process. I thank my sister Elaine for her great organizational skills, my sister Karen Flagg for her endless patience while trying to teach me the art of formatting, and my sister Luann Conine for her enthusiasm, constant praise and positive feedback through the years. Thank you, Beth Royer – the voice of reason with the ability to put my thoughts into words. And I am most grateful for our daughter Jen Groves, who willingly edited my text all times of the day and night, making me look smarter than I am.

Finally, there's my dear husband Charlie who encouraged me to take on this project and has supported me unconditionally through it all. He is my IT guy extraordinaire who tirelessly undoes all the bad stuff that happens while I work at my computer. In addition, over the past three years, he has been there to patiently listen to my endless rambling while I prepared new pizzas, to hold an umbrella over my pizzas as I took them to the grill during the monsoons, and to help me take photos of the finished products. Oh yes, he had to eat more pizzas than I can count. Poor guy, that was a tough job... but someone had to do it! Thanks, Hon.

Table of Contents

Pizza Memoirs ~ Introduction

Food, glorious food ... I can't remember a time in my life that I was not completely captivated by its heavenly aromas, textures, tastes and the feelings which were evoked when consuming anything from the simplest snack to the most elaborate meal prepared with love.

Watching my mother's every move, I was always underfoot in the kitchen; spending countless hours peering over the edge of the chrome trimmed, bright yellow Formica countertop trying to get a glimpse at what she was doing. My mother's cooking was something of a sacred secret to her; a secret that was not willingly shared with many. She would occasionally shoo me away when I got too close to the knife or the hot pot of gravy (tomato sauce) bubbling on the front stove burner, but I was relentless. I learned to cook through observation as mom was a woman of few words when she was frantically preparing meals while simultaneously doing laundry, other household chores and, keeping an eye on my three sisters. I always wanted to tell her how lucky she was that she didn't have to be concerned with my whereabouts when meals were being prepared, but the time never seemed right! Mom didn't appreciate my sense of humor, even in the early days. On some level, I believe my mother understood my love of food; but she worried that it was, at times, the single most important thing in my life. As though to convince herself that it was really nothing to worry about, she would say to me, "I should have known; you were even *born* at dinner time!"

Throughout my childhood, I was painfully shy and over time, I unwittingly developed two coping mechanisms. The first was that I became what teachers lovingly refer to as the class clown; the more anxious I felt, the funnier I became. The second was that I became a really good cook at an early age which allowed me to reach out to people and express my love and caring through the foods I prepared for them. Nothing gave me more pleasure. So why didn't I become a professional chef? Honestly, it never occurred to me because I equated cooking with love, not work or money.

It is funny how things work out in life though. A dear friend died of cancer in the late 1980s, an event which prompted me to become involved with a local hospice program. This work eventually became my second career (the first being a teacher, yes there were a few class clowns with whom I had to contend) and I worked as a hospice pastoral counselor and grief therapist for the next eighteen years. I considered this more of a calling than a job. I truly believed that my patients were living, not dying and I treated them as such. They enjoyed laughing as well as crying with me and the true blessing is that I learned more from the dying than I have ever learned from any living person on this earth.

The two things I brought with me from my youth that helped me to connect on an intimate level with most of my patients were my sense of humor and my love of food. While at Hospice, life review was one of my favorite exercises to do with my end of life patients. This is a simple exercise that basically consists of reminiscing about ones life in an attempt to resolve any unfinished business that needs finishing and healing. Over time I found that simply asking a patient what his or her favorite food was when he or she was a kid was all I needed to do. This usually opened the flood gates and facilitated major healing of old hurts. It is from this work, that I began creating pizzas from the favorite foods of family and friends. Writing **Pizza Memoirs** has been an exercise in uncovering personal histories of family and friends that has enhanced many relationships, deepened previously unexpressed love and facilitated much laughter throughout the entire process.

It is my wish that you will be inspired to begin a journey of your own, talk to family and friends about their favorite foods, discover who they really are and celebrate their lives.

Company's Coming

Those who know me understand how much importance I place on being organized and well prepared when I entertain family and friends. In fact, when describing me, my closest family members and dearest friends tend to use the words 'obsessive' instead of organized and 'compulsive' instead of well prepared. I just ignore them! What I cherish most about entertaining family and friends is spending quality time with them and I find that difficult if I am running around chopping, slicing and dicing ingredients and rummaging through kitchen drawers searching for my zester or some seldom used gadget.

When preparing the pizzas included in this book, having a system that will get you smoothly from the first step in the directions through to the last step is of the utmost importance. There is nothing worse than getting half way through a recipe only to realize that the shredded cheese you need is sitting in the refrigerator in one tightly wrapped hunk, or the butternut squash should have been pre-cooked before making it to the top of your pizza. This is how I avoid those nerve wracking mistakes; I plan ahead. First, I make a double batch of *Surprisingly Simple Pizza Dough*, separate it into six pieces, and place each in a quart size plastic zip top freezer bag that has been labeled with the type of dough, the number of ounces in the piece and the current date.* This dough can be frozen for several months so it is wise to prepare it when you have a free hour or so. Sauce is another important part of your pizza, but who feels like, or has time to make an entire batch of Spanish Sofrito, or marinara sauce if you need only one half cup for your pizza. Again, when I am in the cooking mood, I make sauce and package it in one cup containers; label and freeze them so that all I have to do is take out one container, thaw it and I am good to go. Often times I do this on a Sunday afternoon, otherwise known as, 'sauce Sunday' in our house. It is also practical to prepare in advance other basics like caramelized onions, roasted garlic paste, pesto, and roasted tomatoes, all of which can be frozen according to individual recipe directions. Keeping in mind that your pizza is only as good as the ingredients you use, top quality store bought sauces, pesto, roasted vegetables and the like work well when you are strapped for time.

Now that I have a supply of basic pizza making components in my freezer or on my pantry shelf, I can simply concentrate on preparing and organizing the fresh ingredients needed for the pizza. Read the recipe and decide what you will be able to do ahead. I thaw any sauce and base component, shred cheese and place it into small plastic bags, chop herbs, and pre-cook and refrigerate meats, seafood or poultry. Now this is where my family members begin to throw around the words obsessive and compulsive. Before I begin to assemble the pizza, I place everything on the back of my counter in the order it will be placed on the pizza. Yes, some may find this a bit obsessive, but I find it frees me up to chat and laugh with my family and friends. If truth be told, you can really come off looking like an expert when you deftly grab each ingredient and begin making your pizza. Just be sure that you have the correct order of ingredients or it could get messy.

As with anything you want to do well, pizza making takes a bit of practice; yet is well within the reach of even the most novice cook. Have fun while you are learning this new skill and laugh at your mistakes. Aside from putting huge holes in the center of my almost perfectly shaped dough, my biggest mistake was forgetting the finishing touches. I cannot tell you how many times my guests took that first wonderful bite of pizza only to be stopped dead in their tracks by my somewhat urgent shout, "Wait, I forgot to finish it!" Over time, I have forgotten to spoon the béchamel over the eggs, to drizzle the rich balsamic sauce over the 'antie'pasto and to place delicious dollops of the smoked poblano crema on Janos' grilled mushroom and chili pizza. Although the finishing touches complete the other tastes and textures of your pizza, it is not worth startling everyone just because said touches have been eliminated in error. Calmly excuse yourself from the table, garnish the pieces remaining on the serving board and smile apologetically. I can guarantee that your guests will be more appreciative.

***TIP**: *Leave a small opening at the top of the bag and press the air out with your hand before sealing.*

Equipped For Success

When my mother made dough for her wonderful yeast breads, she had a measuring cup, a bowl, a big wooden spoon (which doubled as a paddle when we did something she didn't like!) and a board on which to knead and shape her dough into breads and fantastically fragrant cinnamon rolls. Even though you can make an amazingly good yeast dough with only a few of the simplest kitchen utensils, having some basic tools of the trade can make life so much easier when it comes to making that dough and turning out a perfect pizza every time. Think of this as your wish list, adding tools as your enthusiasm for pizza making grows.

Gas Grill / Oven that heats to 500° F.

Pizza Grill / Quarry tiles or a pizza stone for the oven when baking pizzas indoors. I recommend the Charcoal Companion PizzaQue Stone Grill®.

Scale – I find that weighing ingredients is much more accurate than using measuring cups when making pizza dough, as flour can be compacted in its container. If you must use measuring cups, fluff the flour first then spoon it lightly into the cup and level it off with the back of a knife. I also find it easier to use a scale for weighing topping ingredients like cheese.

Glass measuring cup – 2 to 4 cup size.

Instant read thermometer – This is very useful when dissolving yeast granules in water that needs to be 110° to 115° F. It is important not to guesstimate the optimal water temperature because if the water is too hot, it can kill the yeast; if it is too cool, it will slow down the development of the yeast. Since I leave nothing to chance, I always have my instant read thermometer handy.

Mixing bowls – I like earthenware bowls, but you can use glass, stainless steel or whatever you have on hand. It is helpful to have a large bowl for dough rising and several small bowls for preparing and storing your pizza ingredients in advance.

Electric mixer – with a paddle for mixing and a dough hook for kneading. My heavy duty KitchenAid® mixer is a true work horse that has never let me down. I must admit though, I now make all my dough with my food processor.

Food processor – These machines never cease to amaze me. I recommend a heavy duty, large capacity machine with a dough blade. It takes only minutes to mix dough ingredients and one to two additional minutes to knead the dough. This is truly revolutionary – especially to anyone who has ever tried to make dough using only a bowl, wooden spoon and good old-fashioned elbow grease.

Mezzaluna – This versatile kitchen utensil has a single or double, very sharp curved blade with a handle on each end. The curve of the blade resembles a half moon, or 'mezzaluna' in Italian. Mezzalunas come in varying sizes; small ones are great for chopping herbs and the large ones are sometimes used to cut pizzas. The ideal chopping surface is a concave board, but any wooden cutting board will suffice. To safely use your mezzaluna, grasp firmly by both handles and carefully rock the device back and forth across your herbs or vegetables. Although I do have a few rather large cutting boards, I prefer using the mezzaluna with its small concave board when chopping herbs to avoid permanently staining my large boards.

Rolling pin – Pizza dough can be flattened with your fingers and stretched into shape all by hand. Should you prefer to roll your dough into shape, I recommend using a long French rolling pin which is a thin, hardwood cylinder with tapered ends that has some good weight to it. A standard rolling pin can also work if that is your preference.

Pastry brush – An indispensable tool for evenly distributing oil over pizza dough before baking and for brushing the outer rim of crust after removing pizza from grill or oven; a simple step that assures a beautifully glistening crust.

Grater – Microplane® graters are quite versatile for finely grating anything from hard cheese and citrus zest to ginger and nutmeg. I limit my use of box graters to using the large holes for shredding softer cheeses like mozzarella.

Pizza peel – A flat, wooden or metal tool that looks like a shovel, the pizza peel has a long handle and facilitates transferring your assembled pizza to and from the grill or oven. You can also use a rimless baking sheet for this job, but the absence of a handle can make transferring your pizza a bit tricky.

Pizza cutter – Whether you use a wheel type or a mezzaluna as described above, be sure to purchase something that is sturdy and that fits well in your hand(s).

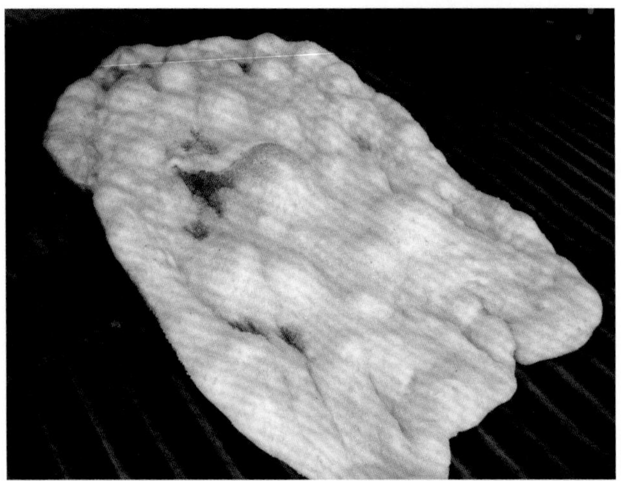

Grilled Pizza Primer

Let's talk about life altering experiences. Grilling pizza is at the top of my list! Having grown up in a very Italian household, the idea of putting a piece of pizza dough anywhere other than into an extremely hot oven was as foreign as swimming in Long Island Sound in the middle of January....you just didn't do it. Grilling your pizza directly on the grates of a gas grill infuses it with the smokiness one would only expect to taste in a brick oven baked pizza. I guarantee that you will not believe how easy it is to grill your pizza.

Gas Grill Preparation

Preheat all burners of your gas grill on high for 10 to 15 minutes with the lid down. Lower the heat in the center of grill (3 or 4 burner grill) or the front burner (2 burner grill) to low just before placing pizza dough on grate. Dough should grill directly over low heat. If using a two burner grill, you will have to rotate the dough half way through the baking time. Keep in mind that all grills are different and you may find it necessary to turn the other burner(s) to medium at this point in order to avoid incineration of a perfectly good pizza crust. The object is to keep the grill temperature around 500° to 600° F.

Roll, stretch and shape your dough into an unrefined rectangular shape approximately 12 by 14 inches, according to basic directions. It is important to shape the dough to fit onto your grill over the burner that will be turned to low heat as you do not want to char edges that overlap hot burners.

Brush both sides of dough with two tablespoons of the olive oil and place on a large, rimless baking sheet or pizza peel that has been lightly dusted with cornmeal. Carefully lift dough and quickly lay it directly on the grate of the pre-heated grill over the burner that has been turned to low. Close grill lid and grill for 3 minutes; check the crust and, if it is *not* browning too quickly, grill for 2 additional minutes, or until bottom is golden brown with darker grill marks. It is important not to peek at your dough for at least 3 minutes; this will give it ample time for its first rise. Gigantic bubbles may appear on your crust while the first side is grilling; fear not, flatten them with your tongs or let them remain for an interesting presentation and fascinating topic for conversation. Remove crust from grill with tongs and place grilled side up on a flat baking sheet or pizza peel.

Proceed with individual recipe.

Pizza Grill Preparation

For recipes requiring the use of a pizza grill, I recommend the Charcoal Companion PizzaQue Stone Grill®. Follow preheating directions included with your pizza grill.

NOTE: *Many of the recipes included in this book that call for grilling can be baked in a conventional oven or on a pizza grill. See individual recipes for baking options.*

Basic Kitchen Techniques And Tips

Mastering these basic techniques and tips will facilitate consistent results and ease in preparation of the pizza recipes contained in this book.

Cheese and Chocolate

Grate hard cheeses like Parmigiano-Reggiano and Pecorino Romano on a rasp or Microplane® zester/grater.

Shred softer cheeses like mozzarella, fontina and asiago on the large holes of a box grater or in a food processor using the shredding blade.

Shave wide strips off a piece of Parmigiano-Reggiano cheese using a vegetable peeler. If shaving chocolate, warm it a bit by holding it in your clasped hands for a few seconds then shave with a vegetable peeler.

Cleaning Mushrooms

To clean mushrooms, brush off dirt with a dry pastry brush or wipe with a damp paper towel, trim end of stem (if using portabella or crimini mushroom, remove entire stem.) Do not rinse under water as mushrooms will retain moisture and become mushy.

Chiffonade

This is a knife technique used for cutting leafy herbs such as basil or vegetables into long, thin strips. Stack leaves, roll them tightly like a cigar, and then cut crosswise with a very sharp knife. I also use this method for cutting prosciutto, salami or other thinly sliced meat to be used as pizza topping; making the cross cuts ¼ to ½ inch wide. Using your fingertips, gently toss the strips to separate.

Mise En Place

A French phrase meaning 'putting in place', this is a crucial step in making the pizzas in this book. Simply stated – measure, pre-cook, chop, shred and assemble your ingredients before you begin to stretch your pizza dough. Organize, organize, and organize!

Roasting Corn

Brush peeled ear of corn with oil. Sprinkle with coarse salt and freshly ground black pepper. Grill on medium-high heat, turning one quarter turn every 5 minutes until nicely charred (15 to 20 minutes total.) Invert a small bowl and place it in the center of a larger bowl. Stand wide end of cob on small bowl and remove kernels by running a knife along the cob from top to bottom.

Toasting Nuts

To toast nuts such as pine nuts and walnuts, place in a preheated 325° F. oven for 7 to 10 minutes, stirring halfway through time. Watch them carefully to prevent burning. When nuts are fragrant and a light golden color, they are done. You can also toast them in a small preheated skillet over medium heat stirring or shaking pan often for 3 to 4 minutes, or until golden brown.

Reheating Pizza

It took me a while to perfect a way to reheat pizza, not because the crust became soggy or the toppings burned, but because we never had any leftover pizza to reheat. Upon beginning a new weight loss program, portion control became a priority and leftovers regularly appeared in our refrigerator. Not being one to waste a perfectly good slice or two of my delicious pizza, I made numerous attempts at reheating. After several disasters including, but not limited to, soggy crust and burned toppings, I have recently come upon a fool proof way of reheating pizza resulting in yummy, sometimes better than just baked results every time. Heat a heavy skillet (cast iron or non-stick) on medium heat until hot to the touch. Place slices of pizza into the pan and cover pan tightly. Turn heat to the lowest setting and allow pizza to 'bake' in your stovetop oven for 10 to 12 minutes or until heated through. There you have it, perfect results every time.

Doughn't Be Afraid ~ Simply Perfect Pizza Dough

I remember the first time I made pizza dough – what a disaster! I don't know if it was my fear of trying something new, a really bad recipe, or a combination of both. The sweat dripped off my forehead as I fought with the dough, not willing to give up. After several hours of proofing, mixing the dough, waiting for it to rise, punching it down and waiting for it to rise again, I was so spent that the idea of making a pizza was ludicrous. Not to be done in by a ball of pizza dough, I studied the recipe, this time having all my ingredients assembled before I began the process (*mise en place*.) This helped, but the dough was still not to my liking. Several years have passed since my clumsy first attempt at making homemade pizza dough; each time tweaking my recipe just a bit until finally – the perfect, yeasty, silky textured ball of dough sat on my wooden board. Ah, victory is sweet!

Perfect pizza dough is possible every time, using the simple, easy to follow recipes in this chapter. So, *doughn't* be afraid; just go for it.

Roll, Stretch And Shape Your Dough ~ Basic Directions

Allow your dough to relax for at least ten minutes after punching it down. Keep it covered to prevent it from drying out. If your dough has been refrigerated, allow about thirty minutes to one hour for it to come to room temperature.

ROLL: Lightly flour a wooden board or other work surface. Place ball of dough on the prepared surface and lightly press with your fingers to slightly flatten it out, working from the center to the edges and rotating dough as you go. Roll dough from the center outward with a rolling pin until it is approximately ½ inch thick; adding flour to the surface and your rolling pin as needed. If dough resists and pulls back, cover it and allow it to rest for another ten minutes. With your fingertips, press around the entire edge of dough approximately one half inch in to form the rim. Keep in mind that rolling the dough will press out some of the air bubbles that give it great texture, so you may choose to flatten dough entirely with your fingertips.

STRETCH: Be sure to remove any 'bling' from your fingers before you begin to avoid poking unwanted holes in your dough. Lift dough and, placing both your hands, knuckles up, under center of dough, gently stretch by moving your hands apart toward outer edges of dough. Rotate dough and repeat. At this point, you can gently grasp dough by the edge and work your way around the perimeter, allowing the weight of the dough to do the stretching for you.

SHAPE: Once your dough is approximately ¼ inch thick, place it on a pizza peel or rimless baking sheet that has been lightly dusted with cornmeal and adjust the shape if necessary. Proceed with individual pizza recipe. I have long ago given up trying to form a perfectly circular piece of dough on which to place my pizza toppings. Aside from the fact that nine out of ten times, I couldn't get the perfect circle, it looks too commercial. I prefer free form pizzas, whether circular or rectangular in shape.

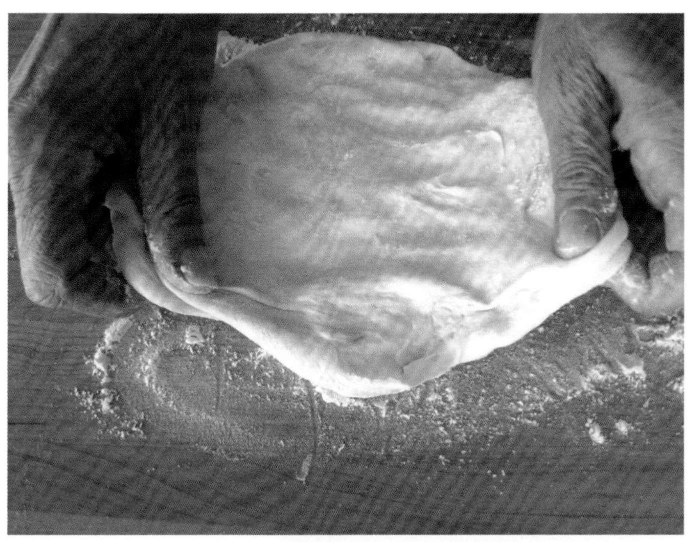

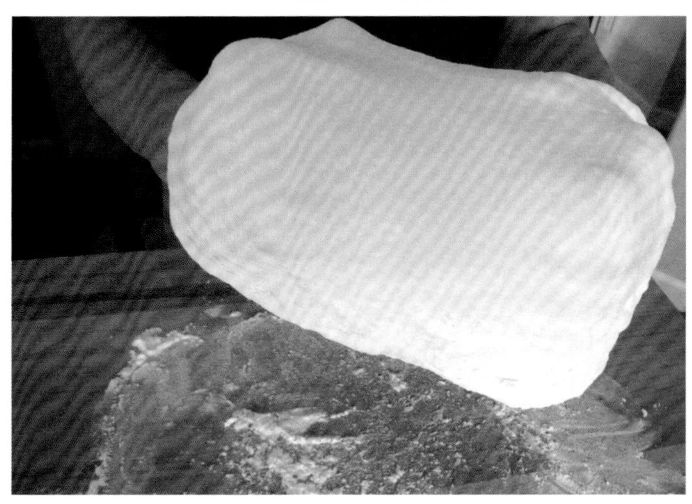

Surprisingly Simple Pizza Dough Food Processor Method

You won't believe how simple it is to make this dough. It has a beautifully smooth texture and wonderful yeasty aroma that brings back memories of long days spent in the kitchen cooking and baking with family.

Although I love Arizona, our tap water leaves much to be desired. I must admit I was spoiled by our icy cold, perfectly tasteless well water in Connecticut. So, I use bottled water in my dough for a clean, fresh taste. If you enjoy drinking your tap water, feel free to use it in your dough.

1 package active dry yeast

1 teaspoon granulated sugar

1¼ cups warm water - approximately 110° F.

3⅓ cups bread flour - approximately 1 pound ¾ ounce (recommended brand - King Arthur's®) plus extra for dusting board

1½ teaspoons kosher salt

1 tablespoon extra virgin olive oil, plus additional for oiling bowl

1. Sprinkle yeast and sugar over warm water in a 2 cup liquid measuring cup; stir with a fork to dissolve. Allow to sit until foamy, about 5 minutes.
2. Add flour and salt to the large bowl of a food processor fitted with a dough blade. Pulse 2 to 3 times to combine.
3. Stir olive oil into the yeast mixture and, with the machine running, slowly pour mixture through the feed tube allowing flour to absorb liquid as you pour.
4. After dough forms a ball, process for one minute longer to knead. Turn out onto a very lightly floured board or counter and shape into a ball.
5. Lightly coat a large earthenware bowl with olive oil. Place dough in bowl and turn dough over to coat with oil. Cover bowl with plastic wrap and set aside to rise in a warm place for 40 to 50 minutes or until doubled in bulk.
6. Place dough on lightly floured surface and punch down. This is done by 'punching' your fist into the center of the dough. Then pull and fold the edges of the dough to the center. Turn ball over so bottom is on top. Reshape into a ball, cover with plastic wrap and let rest for 10 minutes. Divide into three equal portions, shaping each into a ball. Dough is now ready to use or you can refrigerate it in separate plastic bags for up to three days. Remove from refrigerator at least 30 minutes before using. You can also freeze the dough and thaw as needed for two hours, unrefrigerated, allowing another hour for dough to reach room temperature. It is recommended that you initially place prepared dough in the refrigerator for several hours before freezing (24 hours is ideal, but not an absolute necessity.)

Yield – Approximately 24 ounces or enough to make three 12 to 14 inch pizzas

This recipe can easily be doubled.

Electric Mixer Method

*Using ingredients for **food processor method**, follow directions below.*

1. Sprinkle yeast and sugar over warm water in a warmed mixer bowl; stir with a fork to dissolve and allow to sit until foamy, about 5 minutes.

2. Attach dough hook to mixer and add 3 cups of the flour, kosher salt and olive oil to yeast/water mixture.

3. Mix for 1 minute on low speed. Add remaining ⅓ cup flour and continue mixing until dough clings to dough hook and pulls away from sides of bowl. Knead for 2 minutes, turn out onto a lightly floured board or work surface and shape into a ball.

4. Follow steps 5 and 6 for *Surprisingly Simple Pizza Dough*, food processor method.

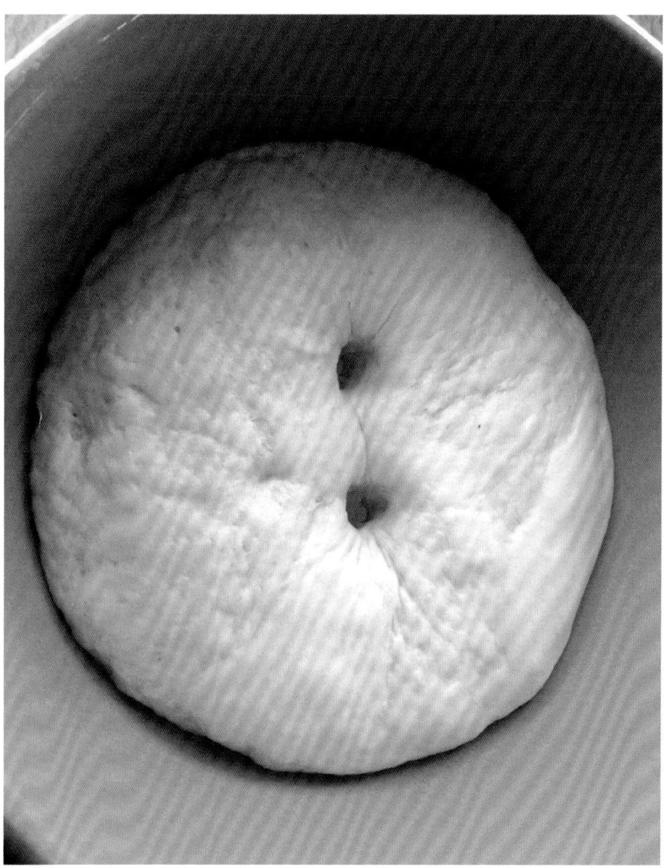

Tip

To test for 'doubled in bulk', quickly press two clean fingers about ½ inch into the top of the dough. If the indentations remain when you pull your fingers out, it is doubled in bulk. If the indentations immediately fill in, allow dough to rise about 15 minutes longer and test again.

Wholesome Whole Wheat Pizza Dough Food Processor Method

This dough has a wonderfully yeasty fragrance, a nutty taste, and a slightly chewy texture. Use it in place of Surprisingly Simple Pizza Dough for the added health benefit derived from the whole grain flour

1 package active dry yeast

1 teaspoon granulated sugar

1¼ cups warm water - approximately 110° F.

1⅓ cups bread flour (recommended brand – King Arthur's®) plus extra for dusting

2 cups whole wheat flour (recommended brand – King Arthur's®)

1½ teaspoon kosher salt

2 tablespoons extra virgin olive oil, plus more for oiling bowl

1 Sprinkle yeast and sugar over warm water in a 2 cup liquid measuring cup; stir with a fork to dissolve. Allow to sit until foamy, about 5 minutes.

2 Add bread flour, whole wheat flour and salt to the large bowl of a food processor fitted with a dough blade. Pulse 2 to 3 times to combine.

3 Add olive oil to the yeast mixture and, with the machine running, slowly pour mixture through the feed tube allowing flour to absorb liquid as you pour.

4 After dough forms a ball, process for one minute longer to knead. Turn out onto a very lightly floured board or counter and shape into a ball.

5 Lightly coat a large earthenware bowl with olive oil. Place dough in bowl and turn dough to coat with oil. Cover bowl with plastic wrap and set aside to rise in a warm place for 40 to 50 minutes or until doubled in bulk.

6 Place dough on lightly floured surface and punch down. This is done by 'punching' your fist into the center of the dough. Then pull and fold the edges of the dough to the center. Turn ball over so bottom is on top. Reshape into a ball, return to oiled bowl and cover with plastic wrap; let rise another 45 minutes. Turn dough out onto a lightly floured surface, punch down, shape into a ball. Cover with plastic wrap and let rest for 10 minutes. Divide dough into three equal portions, about 9 ounces each.

7 Dough is now ready to use or you can refrigerate it in separate plastic bags for up to two days. Remove from refrigerator at least 30 minutes before using. You can also freeze the dough and thaw as needed for two hours, unrefrigerated, allowing another hour for dough to reach room temperature. It is recommended that you initially place prepared dough in the refrigerator for several hours before freezing (24 hours is ideal, but not an absolute necessity.)

Yield – Approximately 24 ounces or enough for three 12 to 14 inch pizzas.

Dessert Pizza Dough Food Processor Method

This is basic, sweetened pizza dough that has a beautifully smooth texture. Adding sugar, citrus zest, cocoa, and /or spices to a plain pizza dough transforms it into a perfectly flavored crust for your favorite dessert pizza.

- **1 package active dry yeast**
- **1 teaspoon granulated sugar**
- **1¼ cups warm water - approximately 110° F.**
- **3 ⅓ cups bread flour approximately 1 pound ¾ ounces, plus extra for dusting (recommended brand - King Arthur's®)**
- **1 teaspoon kosher salt**
- **1 tablespoon raw sugar (turbinado)**
- **1 tablespoon extra virgin olive oil, plus additional for oiling bowl**
- **citrus zest, cinnamon, nutmeg, cardamom, cocoa powder as per individual recipe**

1. Sprinkle yeast and granulated sugar over warm water in a 2 cup liquid measuring cup. Stir with a fork to dissolve. Allow to sit until foamy, about 5 minutes.
2. Add flour, salt and raw sugar to the large bowl of a food processor fitted with a dough blade. Pulse 2 to 3 times to combine. Add any additional zest or spices called for in particular recipes. Pulse 2 to 3 times to combine. Keep in mind that this recipe makes enough dough for two to three dessert pizzas; you may choose to knead the zest and/or spices into individual pieces of dough just before assembling your pizza instead of adding them in this step.
3. Add olive oil to the yeast mixture and, with the machine running, slowly pour the mixture through the feed tube allowing flour to absorb the liquid as you pour. After dough forms a ball, process for one minute longer to knead. Turn out onto a very lightly floured board or counter and shape into a ball.
4. Lightly coat a large earthenware bowl with olive oil. Place dough in bowl and turn dough to coat with oil. Cover bowl with plastic wrap and set aside to rise in a warm place for 40 to 50 minutes or until doubled in bulk. (See Surprisingly Simple Pizza Dough)
5. Place dough on lightly floured surface and punch down. This is done by 'punching' your fist into the center of the dough. Then pull and fold the edges of the dough to the center. Turn ball over so bottom is on top. Reshape into a ball, cover with plastic wrap and let rest for 10 minutes. Divide into two or three equal portions, shaping each into a ball. Dough is now ready to use or you can refrigerate it in separate plastic bags for up to two days. Remove from refrigerator at least 30 minutes before using. You can also freeze the dough and thaw as needed for two hours, unrefrigerated, allowing another hour for dough to reach room temperature.

Yield – Approximately 24 ounces or enough to make three thin 12 to 14 inch pizzas.

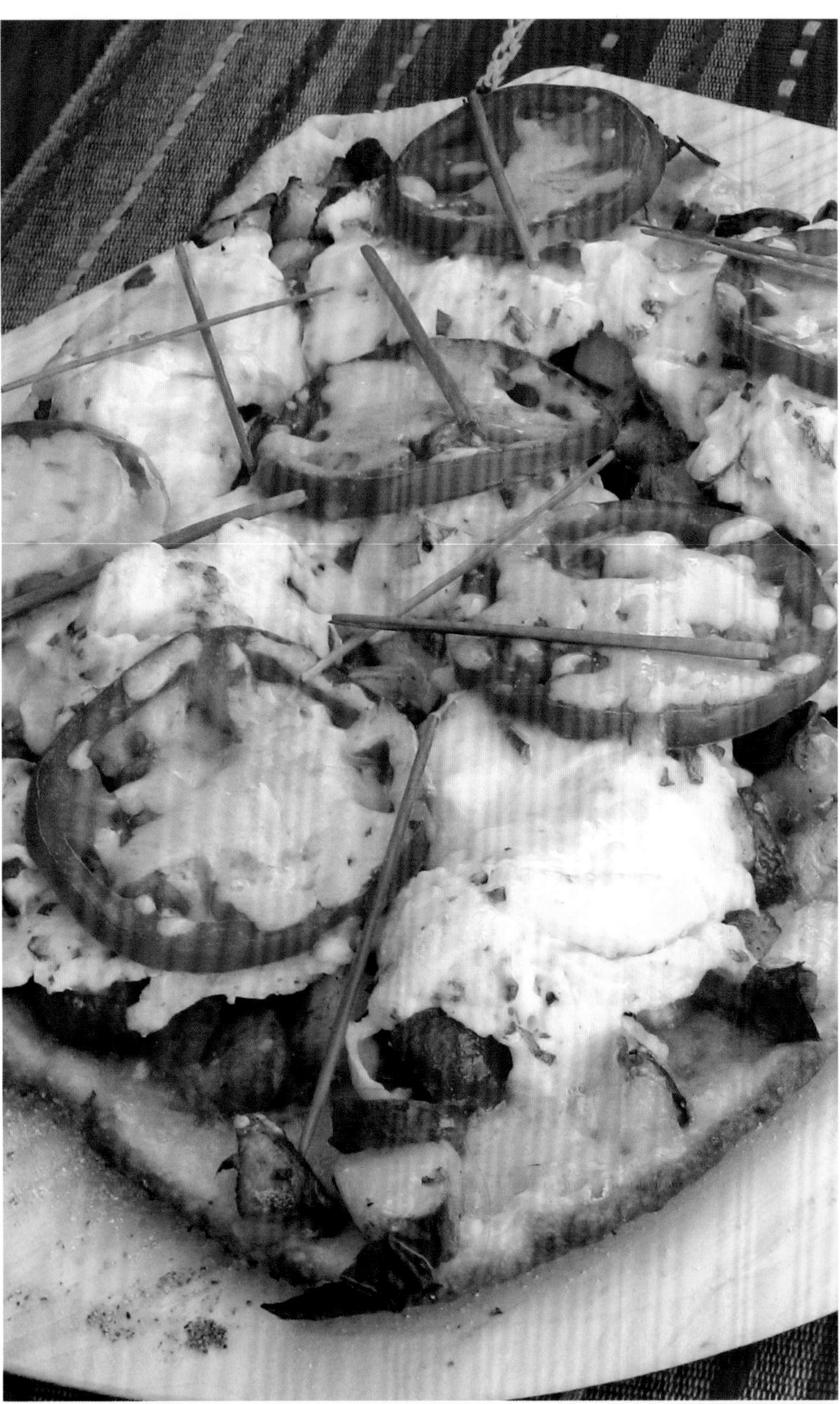

Breakfast Pizzas

Breakfast pizzas are a special treat. My favorite time to make them is on holidays like Mother's Day, Father's Day, or New Years Day when restaurants in our area tend to be overly crowded and it becomes more of a hassle than a pleasure to be out for breakfast.

Last Mother's Day my husband and I invited our good friends Gary and Judi for breakfast. Our children are grown and living out of state so we were all on our own to celebrate as we chose. We all agreed that it would be more relaxing to stay home, chill out (not an easy thing to do in Arizona) and share a breakfast pizza on yet another beautiful spring morning. The only snag – I am the pizza maker in our family. This called for compromise since; after all, it was Mother's Day, my day to be waited on and pampered. The compromise came quickly. My husband agreed to make and serve ice cold mimosas while I prepared *Jen and Colleen's Croque Madame Pizza* and Judi set the table in the shade of our ramada. We talked and laughed for hours; enjoying each others company and a perfectly prepared pizza. What could be a better way to celebrate?

If you are having trouble with the idea of serving pizza for breakfast, I can tell you that the pizzas in this section are equally delicious when served for lunch or dinner. However, I strongly recommend you put your fears and preconceptions aside and make one of these fabulous pizzas for breakfast. Whether you prepare your breakfast pizza on a holiday or on a weekend morning when you just want to slow the pace of your life, you can rest assured that it will be a huge hit with your family and friends.

Aloha Café Breakfast Buffet Pizza

My wonderful husband recently took our family on a week long cruise around the Hawaiian Islands to celebrate our 40th wedding anniversary. What a trip it was! We were excited and open to all experiences that came our way, especially those of us who were 'novice cruisers'. We appreciated the simple beauty of our ship, The Pride of America and the natural beauty found on each of the islands we visited. The most awesome experience, though, was the first time we attended the Aloha Café breakfast buffet. I was taken aback by the variety of foods offered and the amazing presentations of said food, but mostly by the massive amounts of food I saw heaped on 'cruisers' plates. It was truly overwhelming to witness the excess. Having been on my soap box about portion control for several months prior to our cruise, I had to restrain myself and refrain from piling food onto my plate each morning. This pizza represents a blurred image I have of plates gone by. Eat as many pieces as you can; follow that up by consuming three or four huge cinnamon rolls; close your eyes and you are at the Aloha Café Breakfast Buffet!

- **1 recipe Roasted Red Potatoes (recipe follows)**
- **3 tablespoons unsalted butter, divided**
- **¼ cup minced yellow onion**
- **6 slices center cut bacon**
- **4 to 6 fully cooked breakfast sausages – recommended brand Jimmy Dean®**
- **6 extra large eggs**
- **3 tablespoons milk or half-and-half**
- **freshly ground black pepper**
- **1 tablespoon flat Italian parsley leaves, chopped**
- **1 tablespoon fresh chives, chopped plus extra for garnish**
- **9 ounces prepared pizza dough at room temperature**
- **2 tablespoons extra virgin olive oil**
- **6 ounces sharp cheddar cheese, shredded and divided**
- **1 tomato cut into small dice and patted dry on paper towels**
- **kosher salt and freshly ground black pepper to taste**

1. Prepare Roasted Red Potatoes. When cool, cut into small dice and set aside.
2. Melt 2 tablespoons of the butter in a medium skillet over medium high heat. Add onion and cook, stirring for 3 minutes or until onion is translucent. Add diced potatoes to skillet. Cook, stirring occasionally for 4 minutes or until potatoes begin to brown. Using a slotted spoon, remove mixture from skillet and place on a paper towel lined plate to drain. Set aside for topping.
3. Stack bacon slices, cut in half lengthwise then crosswise into ½ inch pieces. Sauté in a medium skillet over medium high heat until fat has been rendered and bacon is just beginning to brown. Remove with a slotted spoon to a paper towel lined plate. Reserve pan with bacon fat for cooking eggs. Slice breakfast sausages crosswise into ¼ inch pieces and set aside with bacon for topping.
4. Place eggs and milk or half-and-half into a bowl. Add freshly ground pepper to taste and whisk until thoroughly combined. Stir in 1 tablespoon cold diced butter, parsley and chives. Use the same skillet in which you cooked the bacon, adding butter if needed to soft scramble the eggs over medium heat for 1 to 2 minutes. Do not overcook the eggs at this point. Cover pan and set eggs aside for topping.
5. Roll, stretch and shape dough into a 12 to 14 inch rectangular or circular shape according to basic directions. Brush dough with olive oil and sprinkle with one half of the cheese. Top with potato-onion mixture, sausage slices and bacon pieces.
6. Bake on a preheated Pizza Grill or on a pizza stone in a preheated 500° F. oven, rotating after 4 minutes to prevent sticking. Bake for 8 minutes, open grill lid or oven and remove pizza to a pizza peel or rimless baking sheet. Immediately close grill lid or oven door so as to not let heat escape. Spoon warm eggs over pizza and arrange tomatoes over the eggs. Top with remaining cheese.

7 Return to grill or oven and bake for 2 to 4 minutes longer or until crust is firm, eggs are warmed and cheese is melted.

8 Remove from heat, season with kosher salt and freshly ground black pepper; garnish with chives. Cut into large squares and serve.

Roasted Red Potatoes

- **1 pound small red potatoes, washed, dried and halved**
- **2 tablespoons extra virgin olive oil**
- **½ teaspoon kosher salt**
- **½ teaspoon freshly ground black pepper**
- **1 teaspoon fresh rosemary needles, minced**

1 Preheat oven to 400° F.

2 Place potato halves on a rimmed baking sheet and drizzle with olive oil.

3 Sprinkle with salt, pepper and rosemary. Toss to coat evenly.

4 Roast 25 to 35 minutes, shaking pan once or twice. Bake until lightly browned and cooked through. Set aside to cool.

HELPFUL HINT: *Make a double or triple batch for dinner the night before and use the leftovers on your breakfast pizza.*

English Fry-Up Pizza

Breakfast at a local pub on our trip to London was not what we expected – and that is an understatement! We found ourselves in a 'greasy spoon', rubbing elbows with mostly locals – messengers, construction workers and the like. After some friendly conversation, it was suggested that we order a traditional English breakfast. We did, and shortly after were presented with plates full of sausages, bacon, eggs, mushrooms and baked beans....not to mention the sides! I just stared at my plate, feeling a bit overwhelmed and wondering - 'what's up with the baked beans?' We were told this breakfast would cure a hangover and get you set up for a long day of hard manual labor. I wouldn't know about the hangover cure, but I probably could have worked a twelve hour day on a construction site without feeling the slightest twinge of hunger. If you want to have a go at a traditional English fry-up without having to go to London for the experience, this pizza is for you.

3 tablespoons extra virgin olive oil, divided

6 ounces pork breakfast sausages (good quality, fresh)

4 strips center cut bacon (rashers)

⅓ cup tomato sauce – recommended brand – Hunt's®

9 ounces prepared pizza dough at room temperature

6 ounces extra sharp cheddar cheese, shredded and divided

½ cup baked beans, drained - recommended brand – Heinz®

4 large eggs

1 tomato, cut into ¼ inch thick slices; drained on paper towels

kosher salt to taste

freshly ground black pepper to taste

1 Heat 1 tablespoon of the olive oil in a medium skillet over medium-high heat. Add sausages and cook, turning frequently for about 10 minutes or until nicely browned. Add bacon to the same pan and sauté along with the sausages for about 4 minutes or until most of the fat has been rendered. Remove sausages and bacon to a paper towel lined plate. As soon as bacon is cool enough to handle, cut or crumble into small pieces. Cut sausages crosswise into ½ inch slices and set aside with bacon for topping.

2 Toss mushrooms into same skillet and sauté for about 3 to 5 minutes or until they are just beginning to brown. Remove with slotted spoon and reserve for topping.

3 Roll, stretch and shape dough into an unrefined 12 to 14 inch square or circular shape according to basic directions. Brush both sides of dough with the remaining 2 tablespoons of olive oil and place on a large, rimless baking sheet or pizza peel dusted with cornmeal. Carefully lift dough and lay it on the preheated grill (see Grilled Pizza Primer.) Close grill lid and grill for 3 to 5 minutes or until bottom of crust is golden brown with darker grill marks. Remove from grill with tongs and place grilled side up on a flat baking sheet or pizza peel. Spread grilled side of dough with an even layer of the tomato sauce.

4 Sprinkle half of the cheese over the sauce and top evenly with sausage, bacon pieces, and mushrooms. Scatter baked beans on pizza then place tomato slices around top of pizza leaving enough room for the eggs. Top pizza with more cheese reserving a bit to place on each egg near the end of baking.

5 Carefully slide pizza onto grill, turning burner directly under pizza to low. Close lid and bake for 5 minutes. Check bottom of crust by lifting the edge with tongs. If it is browning too quickly, turn off burner directly under pizza and continue baking for 1 minutes or until crust is firm and golden, and cheese is melted. Meanwhile, fry four eggs in the skillet in which you sautéed the mushrooms; cover and set aside to keep warm. Place eggs on pizza, being sure to space them evenly, about 1 minute before removing pizza from grill. Top eggs with additional cheese, close grill lid and finish baking the pizza.

6 Remove from heat and season with salt and pepper. Cut into 4 equal wedges or squares, being sure each piece contains a full egg. Serve immediately.

Jen and Colleen's Croque Madame Pizza

After arriving in Paris on a red-eye flight from NY, my daughter Jen and her friend Colleen quickly checked in to their hotel and set out to see the city. They wandered around for several hours looking for the Eiffel Tower which, as you know is pretty hard to miss – especially for two 'Yalies' who were by then both attorneys. Exhausted from walking, they decided to stop at a charming café just ahead. Imagine their surprise when they sat at an outdoor table and looked up to see the tower looming over them at the end of the block. DUH! When recounting this story, they focus not on the elusiveness of the tower, but rather on the fabulous Croque Madame and café au lait they each hungrily consumed. I smile every time I make this pizza and think of the misguided Parisian adventures of Jen and Colleen.

9 to 10 ounces prepared pizza dough at room temperature

1 tablespoon fresh tarragon leaves, chopped; plus extra for garnish

3 tablespoons canola or other vegetable oil, divided

1 slice fresh pineapple, cored and cut ½ inch thick

½ to 1 cup Dijon Béchamel Sauce (page 167) plus extra for finishing

6 ounces Gruyere cheese, shredded and divided (approximately 1½ cups)

4 ounces baked ham, thinly sliced and cut into ½ to ¾ inch wide strips

4 large eggs

kosher salt and freshly ground black pepper to taste

Tip

If using regular baked ham, cut strips ½ inch wide; if using thinly sliced deli ham, cut into ¾ inch strips.

Crack each egg into a small cup before slipping onto the pizza.

1. Knead tarragon leaves into pizza dough and set aside.
2. Brush both sides of pineapple slice with ½ to 1 tablespoon of the oil and grill over medium-high heat until softened and well marked, about 3 to 4 minutes per side. Remove from grill; cut into small dice and set aside for topping.
3. Roll, stretch and shape dough into an unrefined 12 or 13 inch square or circular shape according to basic directions. Brush both sides of dough with remaining oil and place on a large, rimless baking sheet or pizza peel that has been dusted with cornmeal. Carefully lift dough and lay it on the preheated grill (see Grilled Pizza Primer.) Close grill lid and grill for 3 to 5 minutes or until bottom of crust is golden brown with darker grill marks. Remove from grill with tongs and place grilled side up on a flat baking sheet or pizza peel.
4. Spread grilled side of dough with ½ to 1 cup room temperature béchamel sauce, using just enough to coat dough evenly. Keep remaining sauce warm for garnish. Sprinkle about one half of the Gruyere over the sauce and scatter the ham strips and pineapple bits over all.
5. Top with remaining cheese. Using the back of a large spoon, make four wells in the cheese, one on each quadrant, and slip one egg into each well, being careful not to break yolks or let white spread outside of wells. [Alternatively, you can sauté the eggs in butter in a medium skillet while pizza is baking, then add them to the top of the baked pizza.]
6. Carefully slide pizza onto grill, turning burner directly under pizza to low. Close lid and bake for 5 minutes. Check bottom of crust by lifting the edge with tongs. If it is browning too quickly, turn off burner directly under pizza and continue baking for 5 to 7 minutes or until crust is firm and golden, eggs are set and cheese is melted.
7. Remove from grill and spoon a bit of warm béchamel sauce over each egg. Season pizza with kosher salt and freshly ground black pepper; garnish with chopped tarragon.

Mateo's Huevos Rancheros Pizza

Nothing says breakfast like Huevos Rancheros, especially if you are fortunate enough to find a nearby restaurant that serves authentic Mexican food. When our son Matthew visits us he can't seem to get enough Mexican food; he can eat huevos rancheros for breakfast, huge burritos for lunch and then choose fajitas for dinner; he never tires of the wonderful Mexican fare found in Tucson. In fact, they call him Mateo at the local Mexican restaurant!

1 recipe Seasoned Black Beans (recipe follows)

¼ cup tomato salsa, mild or spicy

¼ cup tomato sauce – recommended brand – Hunt's®

2 ounces shredded extra sharp cheddar cheese (approximately ½ cup)

2 ounces shredded Monterey Jack cheese (approximately ½ cup)

8 to 9 ounces prepared pizza dough at room temperature

2 tablespoons extra virgin olive oil, plus more for sautéing eggs

4 large eggs

1 small avocado, diced

¼ cup sour cream

fresh cilantro leaves, chopped

hot sauce

1 In a small bowl, combine salsa and tomato sauce; set aside. In another small bowl, combine the cheddar cheese and the Jack cheese; set aside.

2 Roll, stretch and shape dough into an unrefined 12 inch square or circular shape according to basic directions. Brush both sides of dough with olive oil and place on a large, rimless baking sheet or pizza peel dusted with cornmeal. Carefully lift dough and lay it on the preheated grill (see Grilled Pizza Primer). Close grill lid and grill for 3 to 5 minutes or until bottom of crust is golden brown with darker grill marks. Remove from grill with tongs and place grilled side up on a flat baking sheet or pizza peel.

3 Spread the tomato sauce mixture evenly over grilled side of the dough. Sprinkle one half of the cheese mixture over the sauce.

4 Evenly distribute the seasoned beans over the cheese then top pizza with remaining cheese.

5 Carefully slide pizza onto grill, turning burner directly under pizza to low. Close lid and bake for 5 minutes. Check bottom of crust by lifting the edge with tongs. If it is browning too quickly, turn off burner directly under pizza and continue baking for 5 minutes or until crust is firm and golden.

6 While pizza bakes, sauté the eggs in a bit of extra virgin olive oil until they are set to your liking. Keep warm.

7 Remove pizza from heat, carefully place one fried egg onto each quadrant of the pizza. Sprinkle pizza with diced avocado and spoon on small dollops of sour cream. Season with salt and pepper to taste and garnish with cilantro leaves. Cut, being sure each piece contains an egg and serve with hot sauce.

Seasoned Black Beans

2 tablespoons extra virgin olive oil

½ cup finely chopped yellow onion

1 clove garlic, minced

1 cup canned black beans, drained

½ cup diced canned tomatoes with their juice

½ teaspoon cumin

¼ teaspoon chipotle chili powder

kosher salt to taste

1. Heat olive oil in a medium sauté pan over medium heat. Add onion and sauté, stirring often for about 5 minutes or until onion is soft and golden in color. Add garlic, cumin and chili powder; cook and stir for 30 seconds.

2. Stir in beans and tomatoes; bring to a boil before lowering heat to achieve a steady simmer for about 6 to 8 minutes, or until most of the liquid is absorbed. Season with salt to taste and set aside to cool slightly for topping.

VARIATION: Mateo's Nacho Usual Appetizer Pizza

Simply serve this pizza without the eggs and use a bit more sour cream*, avocado, a few sliced black olives, and hot sauce to finish it off after baking. Or get creative and add shredded cooked beef or chicken thighs or chopped cooked shrimp to pizza on top of the layer of seasoned black beans before baking. Finish as above. Enjoy.

*Mix ½ cup sour cream with 2 teaspoons fresh lime juice and a few drops of hot sauce for a tasty topping.

Appetizer Pizzas

I was recently helping my daughter choose appetizers for a cocktail party she was about to host and suggested the ever popular chafing dish favorite – little smoked sausages bobbing in a bubbling hot mixture of grape jelly and chili sauce. "Mom," she said as she rolled her eyes in disbelief, "that's soooo seventies!" Maybe so, but I'll bet several tons of those little smoked sausages have been consumed over the years. Did we never tire of the same old same old? Complacency ruled and many of us were stuck in a rut out of which some, to this day, have not climbed. Well, there is no time like the present to claw your way out of that rut, otherwise known as your comfort zone. File those outdated and overused recipes – better yet – reconstruct them. Turn them into appetizer pizzas. This is your chance to get creative.

Roll and stretch some pizza dough quite thin; give it an irregular rectangular shape. Take the ingredients from your favorite old time appetizer and creatively use them as your pizza topping. Cut it into small squares after baking and there you have it – a fabulous new appetizer.

Included in this section, you will discover many time honored appetizers that are now new and exciting pizzas. Guests will enjoy assembling the pizzas with you or gathering around to watch and keep you company while you do the work. Either way, they will be sure to enjoy these tasty bites. The only problem I have encountered is that once your guests get a taste of that first fabulous appetizer pizza, they are sure to want more. Be prepared for boos and hisses when you cut them off so they will have room for dinner. I do confess that on more than one occasion, I had to make multiple Appetizer Pizzas and forgo making dinner because I couldn't take the pressure!

'Auntie' pasto Pizza

When I think back on my childhood years, I cannot recall a single time that I walked into one of my Italian auntie's houses without immediately being invited to sit down and have something to eat. That's how it was, and to refuse was an insult...a small glimpse into my weight problem! Food was synonymous with love in our family. I hope you love this antipasto pizza and will feel free to add and subtract ingredients, making it your own kind of love.

8 to 9 ounces prepared pizza dough at room temperature

2 tablespoons extra virgin olive oil, plus extra for finishing

½ cup Basil Pesto, see basic recipe or use purchased pesto

½ cup shredded fresh whole milk mozzarella cheese

12 Oven Roasted Plum Tomato halves (page 171)

1 head roasted garlic from Roasted Tomato recipe, chopped

6 strips Caramelized Peppers, cut in half lengthwise (page 116)

¼ cup Italian black oil cured olives, pitted and halved

4 ounces aged provolone cheese, sliced ⅛ inch thick and cut into strips

4 ounces Prosciutto di Parma, sliced thin and cut into slivers

Balsamic Reduction (recipe follows)

1. Roll, stretch and shape dough into an unrefined rectangular shape approximately 12 by 14 inches according to basic directions. Brush both sides of dough with olive oil and place on a large, rimless baking sheet or pizza peel that has been lightly dusted with cornmeal. Carefully lift dough and lay it on the pre-heated grill, turning burner directly under dough to low. (See Grilled Pizza Primer.) Close grill lid and grill for 3 to 5 minutes or until bottom of crust is golden brown with darker grill marks. Remove from grill with tongs and place grilled side up on a flat baking sheet or pizza peel.
2. Spread dough with a thin layer of basil pesto and cover with the shredded mozzarella cheese.
3. Arrange roasted tomatoes, chopped roasted garlic cloves, peppers and olives over top, leaving a half inch border. Arrange strips of provolone over all.
4. Carefully slide pizza onto grill, turning burner directly under pizza to low. Close lid and bake for 5 minutes. Check bottom of crust by lifting the edge with tongs. If it is browning too quickly, turn off burner directly under pizza and continue baking for 5 minutes or until crust is golden and cheese is melted. Top with slivered prosciutto just before removing pizza from grill.
5. Remove from grill and immediately drizzle with balsamic reduction to taste and extra virgin olive oil. Allow pizza to rest for a few minutes. Cut and serve.

NOTE: *This pizza can be baked on a preheated Pizza Grill or on a pizza stone in a preheated 500° F. oven for 10 to 12 minutes. Be sure to rotate pizza after the first four minutes to prevent sticking. If using either of these methods, it is not necessary to brush dough with olive oil.*

Balsamic Reduction - Yield ½ cup

Place 1 cup good balsamic vinegar into a small saucepan. Bring to a boil, then reduce heat to medium-low and simmer until liquid is reduced by one half, about 20 minutes.

Tip

You may use your own choice for toppings such as hot cherry peppers, anchovies, salami or other Italian deli meats; artichoke hearts marinated in oil or jarred eggplant. Any of these toppings would be in addition to the roasted tomatoes which are necessary for a good base for this pizza. I suggest you do not overload your pizza with toppings as you will not be able to enjoy the subtle flavors of each.

Cheese Platter Pizza

I vividly remember the first time I jazzed up my run of the mill cheese platter appetizer by simply adding some walnuts, dried apricots, dates and a small bowl of honey for drizzling to my usual cheese, apples, and assorted breads; our guests ate so much, dinner was hardly necessary. This pizza, cut into small squares, serves equally well as an appetizer or a delightful European type dessert.

10 dried apricots, roughly chopped

12 medjool dates, pitted and roughly chopped

½ teaspoon freshly squeezed lemon juice

pinch kosher salt

2 tablespoons honey

¾ cup water – reserved apricot soaking liquid

1 tablespoon unsalted butter

8 to 9 ounces prepared pizza dough at room temperature

2 tablespoons walnut or canola oil

½ cup walnut meats, toasted and roughly chopped

2 ounces St. Andre triple crème cheese

1 small Granny Smith apple; peeled, cored and cut into very small dice

½ ripe red pear, cored and very thinly sliced

4 ounces Stilton blue cheese, sliced ¼ inch thick

1 Place apricots in a small bowl and cover with 2 cups of boiling water; let sit for 10 minutes then drain off the water, reserving one cup.

2 Combine apricots, dates, lemon juice, salt, honey and ¾ cup of the reserved soaking water in a small saucepan. Cook over medium-low heat, stirring occasionally, until dates soften and mixture comes together. Add butter and stir until it is incorporated into the mixture. Keep warm until ready to use for topping. [This fruit mixture can be made one day before use. Cool, cover and refrigerate. Bring to room temperature before using.]

3 Roll, stretch and shape dough into an unrefined 12 by 14 inch rectangular shape according to basic directions. Brush both sides of dough with the walnut oil and place on a large, rimless baking sheet or pizza peel dusted with cornmeal. Carefully lift dough and lay it on the preheated grill (see Grilled Pizza Primer.) Close grill lid and grill for 3 to 5 minutes or until bottom of crust is golden brown with darker grill marks. Remove from grill with tongs and place grilled side up on a flat baking sheet or pizza peel.

4 Spread the fruit mixture in a thin, even layer over grilled side of dough. Scatter toasted walnuts over the fruit mixture. Place pieces of the St. Andre triple crème cheese over the nuts then scatter apple pieces and arrange pear slices over all. Top with blue cheese slices.

5 Carefully slide pizza onto grill, turning burner directly under pizza to low. Close lid and bake for 5 minutes. Check bottom of crust by lifting the edge with tongs. If it is browning too quickly, turn off burner directly under pizza and continue baking for 5 minutes or until crust is firm and golden and cheese is warmed and slightly melted.

6 Remove from heat and allow pizza to set-up for 1 to 2 minutes; cut into small squares and serve.

Cheesy Pigs-on-a-Blanket Pizza

This delightful appetizer pizza is a combination of my husband Charlie's two favorite appetizers – age old Pigs-in-a-Blanket and Cheese Pennies, a favorite from the seventies. The sweetness of the yellow bells adds a needed counterpoint to the sharp bite of the Parmigiano-Reggiano cheese. If you are up for a bit of nostalgia, this pizza is for you.

8 to 9 ounces prepared pizza dough at room temperature

½ cup freshly grated Parmigiano-Reggiano cheese, plus additional for finishing

¾ cup mayonnaise, recommended brand – Hellman's® or Best Foods®

1 teaspoon dry mustard

2 tablespoons minced sweet onion

6 ounces cocktail franks like Lit'l Smokies®, roughly chopped

1 tablespoons extra virgin olive oil

1 small yellow bell pepper, cored, seeded, and cut into thin strips or rings

4 scallions-white and green parts, ends trimmed and sliced on an angle

1. Knead 2 tablespoons of the Parmigiano-Reggiano into the pizza dough and set aside.
2. In a small bowl, combine the mayonnaise, remaining Parmigiano cheese, dry mustard and minced onion. Set aside or refrigerate if not using immediately.
3. Roll, stretch and shape dough into an unrefined 10 to 12 inch circular shape according to basic directions. Spread dough evenly with mayonnaise/Parmigiano mixture, using only enough to thinly cover dough right up to edge.
4. Scatter cocktail franks over mayonnaise/cheese layer on pizza. Top with yellow pepper pieces and scallions. Grate on additional Parmigano-Reggiano cheese to taste.
5. Bake on a preheated Pizza Grill or on a preheated pizza stone in a 500° F. oven for 10 to 12 minutes, or until top is bubbly and bottom of crust is firm and evenly browned, rotating after 4 minutes to prevent sticking.
6. Remove from heat and grate additional Parmigiano-Reggiano cheese over all. Cut into small squares and serve immediately.

Tip

You can use any extra mayonnaise/cheese mixture to make a few old fashioned 'Cheese Pennies'. Spread a few teaspoons of the mixture on small party rye or pumpernickel bread rounds and broil for 2 to 3 minutes or until lightly browned and bubbly.

Date Night Pizza

One of our favorite appetizers, Bacon Wrapped Blue Cheese Stuffed Dates, was typically reserved for holidays and special occasions. While pondering the practice of producing these tasty parcels so infrequently, the error of my ways became obvious. 'Hmmm...why can't these sweet, pungent, gooey morsels be transformed into a pizza, I mused?' A special night---any night---"date night"!

8 ounces medjool dates, pitted and halved

¼ cup port wine

6 slices bacon

8 to 9 ounces prepared pizza dough at room temperature

3 tablespoons walnut oil, divided

½ cup mascarpone cheese

¼ cup walnuts, toasted, coarsely chopped and divided (page 18)

4 ounces Stilton blue cheese, crumbled

Rich Balsamic Reduction (recipe follows)

1 Place dates in a bowl, cut side up and drizzle port over them. Allow to sit for 5 to 10 minutes. Drain any remaining port and stir into the mascarpone cheese. Set aside.

2 Cook bacon in a medium sauté pan over medium-high heat until most of the fat has been rendered. Do not allow bacon to become crisp. Remove from pan and drain on paper towels. Crumble and set aside for topping.

3 Roll, stretch and shape dough into an unrefined 12 by 14 inch rectangular shape according to basic directions. Brush both sides of dough with 2 tablespoons of the walnut oil and place on a large, rimless baking sheet or pizza peel dusted with cornmeal. Carefully lift dough and lay it on the preheated grill (see Grilled Pizza Primer.) Close grill lid and grill for 3 to 5 minutes or until bottom of crust is golden brown with darker grill marks. Remove from grill with tongs and place grilled side up on a flat baking sheet or pizza peel.

4 Brush grilled side of dough with remaining tablespoon of walnut oil and evenly spread mascarpone cheese to within ½ inch from the edge. Scatter 2 tablespoons of the walnuts, dates (you can quarter the dates if halves are too large) and crumbled bacon over mascarpone and top with crumbled Stilton blue cheese.

5 Carefully slide pizza onto grill, turning burner directly under pizza to low. Close lid and bake for 5 minutes. Check bottom of crust by lifting the edge with tongs. If it is browning too quickly, turn off burner directly under pizza and continue baking for 5 minutes or until crust is firm and golden and cheese is warmed and slightly melted.

6 Remove from heat, sprinkle with remaining walnuts and drizzle with rich balsamic reduction glaze to taste. Allow to rest for a minute or so; cut into small squares and serve. Enjoy your date!

Rich Balsamic Reduction - Yield ½ cup

1 cup good quality balsamic vinegar

2 tablespoon unsalted butter, cut into small dice

1. In a small saucepan, bring balsamic vinegar to a boil. Reduce heat to achieve a slow simmer and continue to cook until mixture is reduced by half. This should take about 15 to 20 minutes.
2. Before removing mixture from heat, whisk in the butter a few pieces at a time. Set aside for topping.

Momma J's "Let it all Hang out Blues" Pizza

Momma J is singing the 'woke up this morning and my pants were tight' blues not because she ate one too many slices of this Blue Cheese BBQ Chicken delight, rather because she had just given birth to their fourth child, a beautiful girl who was their first daughter! Yes, Momma J was very proud indeed. Her reward for a job well done was this pizza created from one of her favorite foods – Buffalo wings with blue cheese.

1/3 cup barbecue sauce – divided, plus more for finishing

1/2 cup shredded, cooked boneless chicken thighs

8 to 9 ounces prepared pizza dough at room temperature

1/2 cup crumbled Stilton blue cheese, plus more for finishing

1 ear corn, roasted and kernels removed from cob or 1/3 cup frozen roasted corn (recommended brand-Trader Joe's®)

1/2 medium red onion, peeled and thinly sliced or cut into small dice

2 to 4 ounces whole milk mozzarella cheese, shredded

1. Combine 1 tablespoon of the barbecue sauce and shredded chicken in a small bowl. Set aside for topping.
2. Roll, stretch and shape dough into an unrefined rectangular shape approximately 12 by 14 inches, according to basic directions. Spread remaining barbecue sauce over dough and sprinkle with blue cheese.
3. Arrange chicken mixture, roasted corn and onion rings or dice over cheese; top with mozzarella cheese.
4. Bake on a preheated Pizza Grill or preheated pizza stone in a 500° F. oven for 10 to 12 minutes, or until crust is firm and golden and top is lightly browned. Rotate pizza after first 4 minutes to be sure it is not sticking. [To grill this pizza, see instructions below.]
5. Remove from heat and drizzle with additional barbecue sauce; sprinkle with additional blue cheese as desired.

Grilled Momma J's Pizza:

1. Roll, stretch and shape dough into an unrefined rectangular shape approximately 12 by 14 inches according to basic directions. Brush both sides of dough with olive oil and place on a large, rimless baking sheet or pizza peel that has been lightly dusted with cornmeal. Carefully lift dough and lay it on the pre-heated grill, turning burner directly under dough to low. (See Grilled Pizza Primer.) Close grill lid and grill for 3 to 5 minutes or until bottom of crust is golden brown with darker grill marks. Remove from grill with tongs and place grilled side up on a flat baking sheet or pizza peel.
2. Brush pizza crust with remaining barbecue sauce and sprinkle with blue cheese.
3. Complete step #3 above.
4. Carefully slide pizza onto grill, turning burner directly under pizza to low. Close lid and bake for 5 minutes. Check bottom of crust by lifting the edge with tongs. If it is browning too quickly, turn off burner directly under pizza and continue baking for 5 minutes or until crust is golden and cheese is melted.
5. Remove from heat and drizzle with barbecue sauce to taste. Sprinkle with additional blue cheese as desired. Allow to sit for 1 to 2 minutes then cut into 16 squares and serve.

Monsoon Mambo Melon-Prosciutto Pizza

Monsoon Mambo...I have danced it many times while darting through the pounding rain, pizza peel in hand, trying to get to the grill while keeping my pizza dry and out of the path of a lightening strike. On this particular day, my wingman, or should I say my umbrella man – my helpful husband Charlie – was out for the afternoon while I entertained four enthusiastic volunteers at my first pizza testing luncheon. The ladies were here to taste test a dinner and a dessert pizza and they were eager to begin the 'work'. But with little warning, the skies opened up within five minutes of their arrival and there we sat looking through the kitchen windows at the first monsoonal rain of the season. The pizza stone was at the ready on the grill, heated to well over 500 degrees, witnessed by the rain spitting off in all directions as it hit the hot grill lid; but I was not about to dance the mambo today – not yet anyway. I prepared a pitcher of Pinot Grigio spritzers, joined my guests at the kitchen table and had a wonderful time getting to know Faith, Judy, Julie and Barbara while waiting out the storm. Because we were all getting hungry and the rain was not letting up, Faith offered to be my wingman and the dance began. While trying to protect the pizza from the wind and rain, we both got a bit drenched; then had a good laugh at the ridiculousness of it all. As comments and critiques on the first pizza slowed, conversation turned to my guests' favorite foods. Faith shared that one of her favorite appetizers is prosciutto and melon, she loves the sweetness of the melon paired with the saltiness of the prosciutto, not to mention the fact that it is quite simple to make and serve. We all immediately agreed that it would make a fabulous appetizer pizza. Serve the Monsoon Mambo Pizza with a chilled pinot spritzer and celebrate Arizona's rainy season.

Basil Vinaigrette (recipe follows)

8 to 9 ounces prepared pizza dough at room temperature

1 teaspoon coarsely ground black pepper

3 tablespoons extra virgin olive oil, divided

2 cloves garlic, minced

6 ounces asiago cheese, shredded

¼ cantaloupe, peeled, seeded and cut into ¼ inch dice (approximately 5 ounces)

4 ounces Prosciutto di Parma, thinly sliced

sea salt

tiny basil leaves

1. Knead black pepper into pizza dough. Roll, stretch and shape dough into an unrefined rectangular shape approximately 12 by 14 inches according to basic directions. Brush both sides of dough with two tablespoons of the olive oil and place on a large, rimless baking sheet or pizza peel that has been lightly dusted with cornmeal. Carefully lift dough and lay it on the preheated grill, turning burner directly under dough to low. (See Grilled Pizza Primer.) Close grill lid and grill for 3 to 5 minutes or until bottom of crust is golden brown with darker grill marks. Remove from grill with tongs and place grilled side up on a flat baking sheet or pizza peel.
2. Brush dough with remaining olive oil and sprinkle with minced garlic. Scatter asiago cheese to within one half inch from edges.
3. Carefully slide pizza onto grill, keeping burner directly under pizza on low. Close lid and bake for 3 to 5 minutes. Check bottom of crust by lifting the edge with tongs. If it is browning too quickly, turn off burner directly under pizza and continue baking for 3 minutes or until crust is golden and cheese is melted.
4. Remove from heat and immediately top with prosciutto strips and melon cubes. Drizzle some of the Basil Vinaigrette over pizza. You will only use a small amount of the vinaigrette; the rest can be refrigerated for up to one week.
5. Finish with a bit of sea salt if desired; then garnish with tiny basil leaves.

Basil Vinaigrette

- **3 tablespoons white balsamic vinegar**
- **¼ cup fresh small basil leaves, packed**
- **1 clove garlic, coarsely chopped**
- **¼ teaspoon kosher salt**
- **¼ teaspoon freshly ground black pepper**
- **½ cup extra virgin olive oil**

1. Place vinegar, basil, garlic, salt and pepper in a blender. Blend to combine ingredients.
2. With the motor running, pour olive oil into the blender in a steady stream. Blend until emulsified (completely combined.)

COOK'S NOTE: *For an amazingly quick and absolutely delicious salad, alternate slices of fresh tomato and slices of mozzarella cheese on a plate, drizzle with Basil Vinaigrette and garnish with fresh basil leaves. Season salad with sea salt and freshly ground black pepper to taste.*

Tip

Roll each slice of prosciutto tightly and cut crosswise into ¼ to ½ inch strips. Separate gently with fingertips.

'Pear'fect Prosciutto Pizza

Kate was diagnosed with stage four lung cancer about four years after her husband died from the same disease. Having witnessed the pain and suffering of her beloved husband, Kate wanted no part of treatments that, in her opinion, would not guarantee her much additional time and/or a good quality of life. I did not have many patients like Kate in that she claimed to be totally prepared and willing to let go of life as she knew it and 'be done with it' as she would often say. She had a wonderful daughter who dedicated herself to taking care of her mother, all the while trying to convince her not to 'give up' so easily. Oftentimes on visits to Kate, I would find her daughter Lizzie at the stove preparing homemade custard for her mother. This became a daily ritual, her way of getting some nourishment into her mother who was refusing most solid foods. When I asked Kate one day if she always loved custard, she quipped, "No, actually I hate the stuff, but it goes down easy." She then told me that what she was really longing for was a few nice juicy pear slices slathered with creamy cheese and wrapped in prosciutto; but she was having difficulty swallowing and was afraid of choking.

Kate was a woman of deep faith who strongly believed that bigger and better things awaited her after her death and she repeatedly refused to explore any spiritual issues with me. As a hospice pastoral counselor, I broached the subject during each visit, always offering to pray with or for her and each time she waved me off with a smile. One beautiful fall afternoon when I arrived at Kate's for a visit, she looked frail and weaker than usual. She agreed that I could pray for her, but only if I did it silently. I had to laugh to myself because she had a stubborn streak that was tempered with humor, making it difficult to take her seriously. Lizzie and I shared a look that said we were wondering why she would choose today to allow prayers to be said for her. Kate drifted off to sleep while her daughter and I quietly prayed, Lizzie wondering if this would be the day that her mother would not awaken from her deep sleep. Approximately thirty minutes later, Kate awoke; sleepily looking around she asked, "Am I dead?" "No", I quietly said to her, "you are very much alive." She looked at us and said, "Oh, shit." Needless to say, the laughs could not be stifled. Kate gave her daughter a reason to laugh even though her heart was breaking. Kate's battle with cancer ended soon after this day, and if, as I believe, prayers are answered, she is in a better place.

I have used the foods Kate was longing for toward the end of her life to create The 'Pear'fect Prosciutto Pizza. In doing this, I honor her strong will, her wonderful sense of humor, and her deep faith and spirituality.

Nothing pairs more perfectly with pears than pungent gorgonzola cheese, salty prosciutto and toasted walnuts; add a touch of sweet honey and you have the 'pear'fect union.

- **2 small pears, Anjou or Bosc, ripe yet firm**
- **3 tablespoons walnut oil, divided**
- **8 to 9 ounces prepared pizza dough at room temperature**
- **4 ounces whole milk mozzarella cheese, shredded**
- **3 ounces Prosciutto di Parma, very thinly sliced and cut into ½ inch strips**
- **2 to 3 ounces gorgonzola or Stilton blue cheese, crumbled**
- **¼ cup walnuts, toasted and broken into pieces**
- **artisanal honey for drizzling – orange blossom or other favorite**

1. Take a thin slice from the bottom of each pear to stabilize it for slicing. Slice pears ⅛ inch thick, cutting from top to bottom of pear. Remove core from each slice with a small spoon, leaving slice intact. Set aside for topping.
2. Roll, stretch and shape dough into an unrefined rectangular shape approximately 12 by 14 inches according to basic directions. Brush both sides with two tablespoons of the walnut oil and place on a large, rimless baking sheet or pizza peel that has been lightly dusted with cornmeal.
3. Carefully lift dough and lay it on the preheated grill (see Grilled Pizza Primer.) Close grill lid and grill for 3 to 5 minutes or until bottom of crust is golden brown with darker grill marks. Remove from grill with tongs and place grilled side up on a flat baking sheet or pizza peel. Brush with remaining one tablespoon walnut oil.
4. Scatter mozzarella evenly over grilled side of the dough; arrange pear slices over the cheese.
5. Carefully slide pizza onto grill, leaving burner directly under pizza on low. Close lid and bake for 6 minutes. Quickly remove from grill to the pizza peel and close grill lid to keep in heat. Scatter strips of prosciutto over all and top with crumbled gorgonzola or blue cheese. Slide pizza back onto grill and turn off burner directly under pizza if crust is browning too quickly. Continue baking for 4 minutes.
6. Using tongs, carefully remove to pizza peel or flat cookie sheet. Sprinkle with walnut pieces and drizzle with honey. Cut into squares and allow pizza to cool for a few minutes before serving.

Entrée Pizzas

Rich memories of seasonal favorites like ripe, red summer tomatoes bursting with flavor served as inspiration for several of the entrée pizzas included in this chapter. I vividly remember sitting on the back porch with my sisters biting into lightly salted, deep red tomatoes like one would bite into a ripe peach, juice running down our hands and arms as we enjoyed each luscious mouthful. Those were simpler times when the ordinary seemed extraordinary.

Memories of special holiday meals shared with family and friends also inspire wonderful pizzas that can easily be prepared any time of the year. Think of the fun you can have when you serve Thanksgiving, Christmas or Easter dinner on a pizza. Who among us does not have a story to share about at least one of those past holiday dinners?

Choose a favorite dinner you enjoyed on a holiday or any day of the week and make it into a pizza. It will take a bit of thought to deconstruct the dinner and reassemble it as a pizza, but the end result will give you great pleasure. In the meantime, look through this chapter and you may find some of your favorite dinners have already been converted to extraordinary pizzas.

Enjoy.

Auntie Ann's Creamy Chick'n Mushroom Pizza

My cousin Kenny described his favorite food as a chicken and mushroom dish his mother, my Auntie Ann, used to make for him. I could almost taste it as he spoke of the 'usual' spices she added and of the garlic. Kenny said, "Everything had garlic as I remember."...a statement that brought me right back to our childhood days. I never thought of Auntie Ann as a great cook because she was very busy running Ann's Newfield Bakery, but Kenny said he "...used to love that chicken served with the 'mandatory' salad containing plenty of olives." My guess is that Auntie Ann would never have imagined that her son's very favorite chicken dish would one day become a pizza. When you make this pizza, don't forget to serve the 'mandatory' salad.

- **1 cup from one can (10 ¾ ounces) cream of mushroom soup – recommended brand Campbell's®**
- **3 tablespoons fresh flat leaf parsley, chopped; plus additional for garnish**
- **¼ teaspoon kosher salt, plus additional for seasoning**
- **½ teaspoon freshly ground black pepper, plus additional for seasoning**
- **4 ounces whole milk mozzarella cheese, shredded**
- **1 (6 ounce) boneless skinless chicken breast or thigh cut into ½ inch strips**
- **¼ teaspoon garlic powder**
- **4 tablespoons extra virgin olive oil**
- **1 tablespoon unsalted butter**
- **3 cloves garlic, chopped**
- **6 ounces white button mushrooms, cleaned and thickly sliced**
- **8 to 9 ounces prepared pizza dough at room temperature**
- **2 ounces St. Andre triple crème cheese cut into ¼ inch slices**

1. In a medium bowl, combine cream of mushroom soup, parsley, salt, pepper and mozzarella cheese. Set aside for topping.

2. About 15 to 20 minutes before preparing pizza, season chicken strips with salt and pepper to taste and garlic powder. Heat 2 tablespoons of the olive oil in a medium sauté pan over medium-high heat. Sauté chicken until it loses its pink color and browns slightly. Remove from pan and when cool enough to handle, cut into bite size pieces. Set aside for topping. Skip this step if using cooked chicken.

3. Add the butter to the pan in which you sautéed the chicken. Heat on medium-high until butter foams. After foam subsides, add garlic and stir a few times. Add mushrooms and season with pepper to taste; toss to combine. Cook for a few minutes undisturbed, then stir occasionally and cook until mushrooms are lightly browned, about 5 minutes. Set aside to cool and use for topping.

4. Roll, stretch and shape dough into an unrefined 12 by 14 inch rectangular or circular shape according to basic directions. Brush both sides of dough with the remaining 2 tablespoons of olive oil and place on a large, rimless baking sheet or pizza peel that has been dusted with cornmeal. Carefully lift dough and lay it on the preheated grill (see Grilled Pizza Primer.) Close grill lid and grill for 3 to 5 minutes or until bottom of crust is golden brown with darker grill marks. Remove from grill with tongs and place grilled side up on a flat baking sheet or pizza peel.

5. Spread soup/cheese mixture evenly over grilled side of dough to within ½ inch from edge. Carefully slide pizza onto grill, turning burner directly under pizza to low. Close lid and bake for 4 minutes, or until soup and cheese begin to melt. Using tongs, carefully remove pizza to a pizza peel; immediately close grill lid. Scatter chicken strips over pizza, top with sautéed mushrooms and St. Andre cheese. Turn off burner directly under pizza. Return to grill and bake for 8 to 10 minutes longer or until crust is firm, topping is bubbling and cheese is melted.

6 Remove from heat and sprinkle with chopped parsley. Cut and serve immediately.

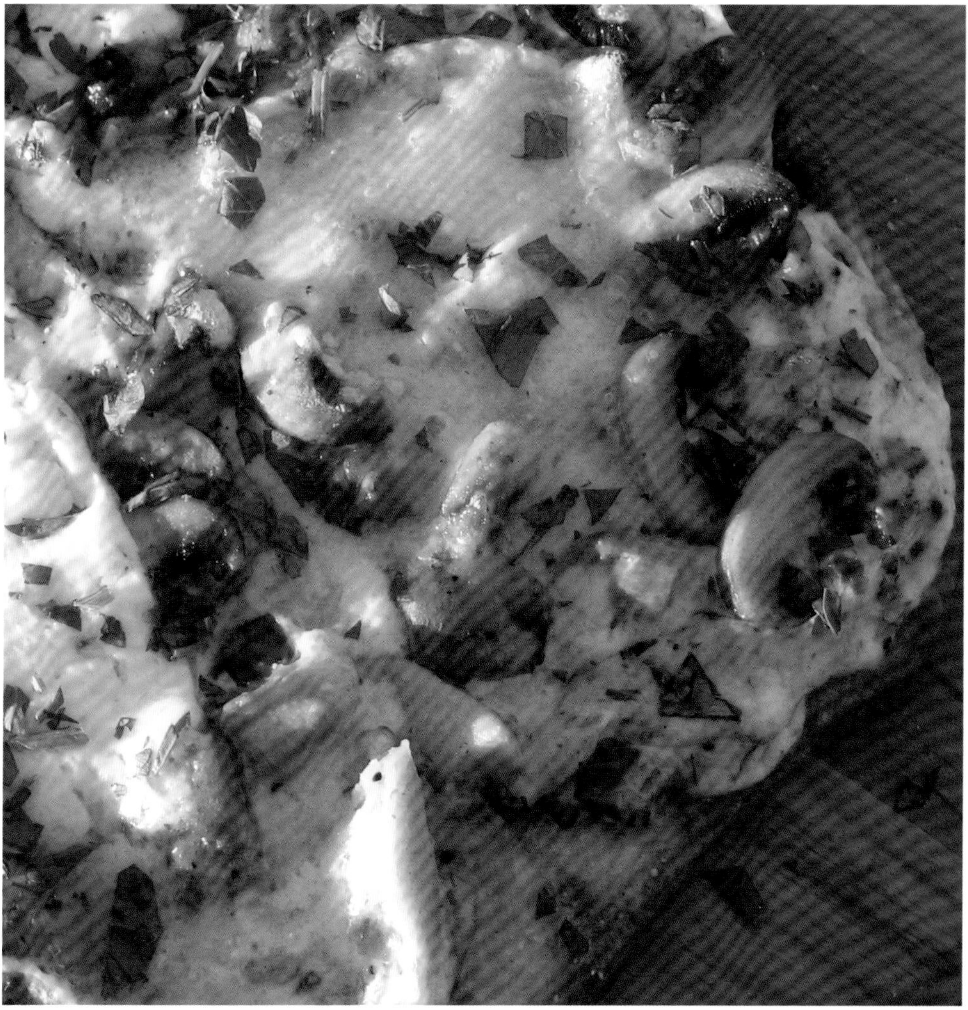

Awesome Autumn Pizza

Today is the first day of fall and it is a toasty 102 degrees here in Tucson, AZ. I find myself missing the sights, sounds and smells of fall in New England. As I sat outside in the heat of the day, I closed my eyes and imagined I was sitting in front of one of the fireplaces in our previous home in CT. I could feel the heat of the fire (of course it was the sun), see the vibrant foliage and hear the crunching of leaves as we buckled down to complete yard work in anticipation of winter. I recalled the bounty of apples and squash, our visits to orchards on crisp fall days and the comfort derived from enjoying a warm galette, bubbling over with fragrant butternut squash, apples and cheese. The Awesome Autumn Pizza is my snapshot of fall in New England.

1 tablespoon olive oil

4 tablespoons unsalted butter, divided

1 small butternut squash (about ¾ pound), peeled, seeded and cut into ½ inch dice

pinch kosher salt

freshly ground black pepper to taste

¼ cup water (more as needed to prevent burning of squash)

pinch freshly ground nutmeg

8 to 10 whole fresh sage leaves, plus additional for garnish

8 to 9 ounces prepared pizza dough at room temperature

1 recipe Caramelized Onions (page 169)

5 ounces Stilton blue cheese or other good blue cheese, divided

6 whole chestnuts, roasted, peeled and chopped – available in specialty stores

1 large baking apple such as Cortland or Granny Smith, cored, halved and cut into ⅛ inch slices

2 teaspoons fresh thyme leaves

maple syrup for drizzling, dark amber grade a is preferred

1 Heat 1 tablespoon olive oil and 1 tablespoon of the butter in a medium sauté pan over medium-high heat. Add squash, salt and pepper and stir to combine. Cook for 3 to 4 minutes or until squash is completely coated with oil/butter mixture and slightly softened. Add water to pan, cover and cook for 5 minutes longer or until softened but not mushy. Using a slotted spoon, remove squash from pan and grate fresh nutmeg over the pieces. Set aside to cool.

2 Melt the remaining 3 tablespoons of butter in a small skillet over medium heat. Add whole fresh sage leaves and cook until butter begins to brown, stirring occasionally. Be careful not to let the butter burn. Remove from heat and set aside to cool.

3 Roll, stretch and shape dough into an unrefined 12 to 14 inch circular shape according to basic directions. Brush dough with browned butter and top with sage leaves, tearing them apart and distributing evenly over dough.

4 Spread caramelized onions out over entire crust, leaving about a ½ inch border. Top with 2 ounces of the Stilton.

5 Scatter butternut squash over entire pizza and top evenly with chestnuts. Arrange apple slices over all.

6 Top with remainder of the Stilton cheese and sprinkle with thyme leaves.

7 Bake on a preheated Pizza Grill or on a preheated pizza stone in a 500° F. degree oven for 10 to 12 minutes, rotating pizza after 4 minutes to prevent sticking. Bake until crust is firm and golden, top is bubbly and apples are softened.

8 Remove pizza from grill or oven and immediately drizzle with maple syrup if desired. Garnish with fresh sage leaves; cut and serve.

NOTE: *This makes a great appetizer pizza if you stretch dough into a 14 inch long rectangular shape. After baking, cut into small squares.*

Tip

To cube butternut squash, cut off top and bottom ends and peel squash with a vegetable peeler. Stand squash on end and slice lengthwise, cutting from top to bottom, into ½ inch planks. Remove seeds as you slice planks. Stack planks and cut lengthwise into ½ inch strips; then cut crosswise into ½ inch cubes.

Benny's Sausage and Peppers Pizza

My father Benny absolutely loved sausage and pepper grinders – the greasier the better! One of my fondest memories of him is of the first time he tasted my sausage and peppers; he smiled, smacking his lips and said, "Deeeelicious, Doll!" This was the highest compliment one could get from him regarding food and I was honored! Every time I bake this pizza, I can picture Benny up to his elbows in grease, savoring every morsel of the sausage and pepper grinders he so loved.

⅓ cup extra virgin olive oil

2 to 3 links sweet Italian sausage (8 ounces total weight)

2 green bell peppers, cored, seeded and cut lengthwise into ½ inch strips

1 medium yellow onion, cut into ½ inch thick slices

1 teaspoon minced fresh rosemary needles or ½ teaspoon dry, crushed

2 cloves garlic, chopped

¼ teaspoon kosher salt or to taste

freshly ground black pepper to taste

8 to 9 ounces prepared pizza dough at room temperature

⅓ cup Marion's Marinara Sauce (page 164)

6 ounces whole milk mozzarella cheese, shredded and divided (1½ cups)

¼ cup Parmigiano-Reggiano cheese, freshly grated

1 Heat the olive oil in a large sauté pan over medium-high heat. Add sausage links and cook, turning frequently, for about 10 to 15 minutes or until browned. [Sausages will finish cooking on the pizza.] Remove links from pan and set aside until cool enough to handle. Cut sausages crosswise into ¼ inch slices; reserve for topping.

2 Add peppers, onions, rosemary, garlic, salt and pepper to same skillet. Lower heat and sauté for 7 to 10 minutes, stirring often until peppers and onions just begin to soften. Remove vegetables from oil with a slotted spoon and set aside to cool for topping. Reserve oil.

3 Roll, stretch and shape dough into an unrefined 10 to 12 inch circular shape according to basic directions. Brush dough with reserved oil. Spread an even layer of marinara sauce over dough and sprinkle with ¾ cup of the shredded mozzarella cheese. Arrange sausage, pepper and onion slices over cheese layer. Top with remaining ¾ cup mozzarella; drizzle with any remaining reserved oil and sprinkle grated Parmigiano-Reggiano over all.

4 Bake on a preheated Pizza Grill or on a preheated pizza stone in a 500° F. oven, rotating pizza after four minutes to prevent sticking. Bake for 10 to 12 minutes or until crust is firm and golden and top is bubbly.

5 Remove from heat; allow pizza to rest a few minutes before cutting into slices. Although I cut most of my pizzas into squares, this is one of those pizzas that taste better if you cut it into more traditional slices; that way you can fold each slice to contain the toppings as you eat it from the tip to the outer edge like a true Italian!

Beautiful Bella

One of my Hospice patients, Bella was a feisty 82 year old Italian woman who was just shy of 5' tall. Although quite frail, she refused to give in to her cancer; "I'm just fine" was her usual response to any inquiries about her health. As the Hospice Pastoral Counselor, I visited her weekly toward the end of her life. Bella was cordial and polite, keeping me at arms length, but I understood that in spite of her bravado, she feared the unknown of her impending death and most likely my weekly visit meant to her that the end was nearing. After I shared with her that I too grew up in a large Italian family, she was more willing to talk to me, yet she tried to keep conversations focused on me and my family, deliberately avoiding divulging any information about her own life.*

In an effort to engage Bella in some meaningful conversation and processing of feelings, I began this particular visit with a story about my father and his love for sausage and pepper grinders, also sharing how much I loved all foods Italian. She smiled and nodded, I knew I had a connection and the time was right to gently press ahead. I said quietly, "Bella, what was your favorite food when you were a kid?" The flood gates opened and she was transported back to her childhood days; recounting memories of her hard working mother who struggled to feed the family when money was scarce. She talked of her favorite meal, escarole and beans, and what a special treat it was when her mother could scrape together a few extra pennies to buy Parmigiano to grate over the top of their bowls full of steaming 'scharole' and beans.

My heart was full one snowy afternoon, when I arrived for my visit only to find Bella standing behind her walker, at the stove stirring a small pot of escarole and beans...loaded with garlic (she remembered that I love garlic.) She saw the concerned look on my face and said, "You made me remember how good this was so I made some for you." We sat and shared a bowl of her 'childhood memory' and six days later Bella's life ended.

At her funeral, I discovered that it was her son who bought the ingredients for the escarole and beans we shared that afternoon. She flatly refused his help in preparing the dish saying to him, "Get out of my kitchen, I was cooking long before you were born." That was Bella, feisty to the end.

It is my guess that Bella would have loved Lucille's Luscious 'Scharole and Beans Pizza ~ Bella's favorite without the bowl.

**My patient's name has been changed to protect her privacy. She was a most beautiful spirit so I called her Bella.*

Bertie's Best Christmas Pizza

Bertie and I have been best friends for more than fifty years! We grew up during a simpler time, in a simply beautiful place on the sound called Lordship. As you can imagine, over the years we have shared many of life's joys and too many of life's sorrows, amassing memories that at times are too numerous to recall. One memory that Bertie has no trouble recalling is of her dad, Albert, flying the family down to Florida for Christmas dinner at the Ocean Grill. Bertie remembers every detail of the wonderful family dinners at the huge round table under the grand chandelier, ordering her favorite dinner – lobster and creamed spinach! I had dinner at the Ocean Grill recently, on her recommendation, and they still serve lobster with creamed spinach. Hopefully, this pizza brings to mind fantastic memories of love and laughter felt at those Christmas dinners of old.

1 recipe Creamed Spinach, recipe follows (makes enough for two pizzas)

3 tablespoons unsalted butter

8 to 9 ounces prepared pizza dough at room temperature

2 tablespoons extra virgin olive oil

¾ cup shredded Gruyere cheese

1 cup lobster meat, cooked

¼ cup Parmigiano-Reggiano cheese

kosher salt and freshly ground black pepper to taste

1. Melt butter in a small skillet and keep warm over very low heat until needed.
2. Roll, stretch and shape dough into an unrefined 12 by 14 inch rectangular or circular shape according to basic directions. Brush both sides of dough with olive oil and place on a large, rimless baking sheet or pizza peel. Carefully lift dough and lay it on the preheated grill (see Grilled Pizza Primer.) Close grill lid and grill for 3 to 5 minutes or until bottom of crust is golden brown with darker grill marks. Remove from grill with tongs and place grilled side up on a flat baking sheet or pizza peel dusted with cornmeal.
3. Spoon approximately one half of the creamed spinach over grilled side of dough, using more or less as desired. Using two forks, spread out creamed spinach evenly, leaving a one half inch border. Sprinkle with Gruyere cheese.
4. Carefully slide pizza onto grill, turning burner directly under pizza to low. Close lid and bake for 5 minutes. Check bottom of crust by lifting the edge with tongs. If it is browning too quickly, turn off burner directly under pizza and continue baking for 5 minutes or until crust is golden and cheese is melted. Meanwhile, sauté lobster in melted butter for about 3 to 4 minutes depending on size of lobster pieces; just long enough to warm it.
5. Remove pizza from grill and immediately arrange lobster pieces over spinach and melted cheese. Top with Parmigiano-Reggiano and season with coarse salt and freshly ground black pepper to taste.
6. Cut into small squares and enjoy "Bertie's Best!"

Tip

If using more than half of the creamed spinach mixture, allow 2 to 4 minutes extra baking time so mixture will heat through and brown.

Creamed Spinach - Yield approximately 4 cups

- **1 cup whole milk**
- **1 cup heavy cream**
- **3 tablespoons unsalted butter**
- **1 medium yellow onion, chopped**
- **3 tablespoons all-purpose flour**
- **1½ teaspoons kosher salt**
- **½ teaspoon freshly ground black pepper**
- **½ teaspoon freshly grated nutmeg**
- **2 (10 ounce) packages frozen chopped spinach, cooked (4 to 6 minutes) drained and squeezed dry**
- **½ cup Parmigiano-Reggiano cheese, freshly grated on a Microplane®**
- **¼ cup shredded Gruyere cheese**

1. Combine milk and cream in a small saucepan and scald. Set aside.

2. Melt butter in a medium sauté pan over medium heat. Add onions and sauté until translucent, about 10 minutes. Stir in flour; cook and continue stirring until completely blended, about 2 minutes. Do not allow flour to brown. Add hot milk and cream mixture, whisking until smooth. Stir in salt, pepper and nutmeg; cook and stir until thickened. Add spinach, Parmigiano and Gruyere cheese; stir to combine and set aside for topping.

MAKE AHEAD TIP: *The creamed spinach can be made ahead. Cool, cover and refrigerate for up to two days. Bring to room temperature before topping the pizza.*

Beth's Bodacious Veggie Bomb Pizza

*My 'niece-in-law' Beth became a vegetarian in the autumn of her 8th grade year after reading Upton Sinclair's **The Jungle**. She remained a pretty solid vegetarian for eight or nine years and then she began adding some fish to her diet. Somehow, living with my nephew and becoming part of our big Italian family has set Beth on a long downhill slide until one evening last year when, after consuming a few too many beers, she decided that sesame-coated chicken fingers looked pretty good! Since then she has been know to occasionally consume a bit of pork, chicken and of course, bacon. I believe this vegetarian pizza tastes "meaty" enough to satisfy the pesky carnivore that playfully taunts Beth from within.*

½ large red onion cut crosswise into ¼ to ½ inch thick slices

½ large yellow bell pepper, cored, seeded and quartered

1 large portabella mushroom cap, cleaned and cut into ½ inch slices

1 medium zucchini, ends trimmed and cut lengthwise into ⅛ inch slices

6 tablespoons extra virgin olive oil, divided

1 teaspoon kosher salt

freshly ground black pepper

8 to 9 ounces prepared Whole Wheat Pizza Dough at room temperature (page 24)

1 tablespoon fresh thyme leaves, chopped

½ cup Roasted Red Pepper Pesto (page 174)

3 ounces Manchego cheese, coarsely shredded

3 ounces whole milk mozzarella cheese, shredded

6 slow roasted tomato halves and ½ head roasted garlic (page 170)

¼ cup pitted black olives (oil cured preferred)

2 ounces fresh, aged goat cheese, crumbled

lemon zest, freshly grated on a Microplane®

fresh baby spinach leaves for garnish

1 Thread onion slices onto 2 parallel metal skewers to hold rings in place and to facilitate turning slices; brush onion slices, pepper, mushrooms and zucchini with 4 tablespoons of the olive oil. Season lightly with salt and ground pepper. Grill over medium-high heat for about 4 minutes per side, or until vegetables are slightly softened and have nice grill marks. Remove from grill and set aside to cool slightly for topping. When bell pepper is cool enough to handle cut into narrow strips. Cut each roasted tomato half in half lengthwise; set aside.

2 Knead chopped thyme leaves into dough. Roll, stretch and shape dough into an unrefined 12 to 14 inch circular or rectangular shape according to basic directions. Brush dough with remaining 2 tablespoons of olive oil and place on a pizza peel or a large, rimless baking sheet that has been dusted with cornmeal.

3 Spread red pepper pesto evenly over dough; top with Manchego and mozzarella cheese. Arrange grilled vegetables, roasted tomatoes, chopped roasted garlic, and olives over all. Top with crumbled goat cheese.

4 Bake on a preheated Pizza Grill or on a preheated pizza stone in a 500° F. oven, rotating after 4 minutes to prevent sticking. Bake for 10 to 12 minutes or until crust is firm and golden and top is bubbly.

5 Remove from grill and top with lemon zest, a handful of baby spinach leaves, and salt and pepper to taste.

HELPFUL HINT: *I usually grill double or triple the amount of veggies needed for this pizza the night before; setting aside enough for the pizza and using the rest for dinner. This step drastically cuts the preparation time on pizza day....always a good thing. Alternatively, you can buy your favorite mix of already prepared roasted vegetables.*

Big Horseradish Twice Baked Potato Pizza

The 'beast' for our Christmas feast is always a large, luscious roasted prime rib of beef with creamy horseradish sauce. The feast also includes a casserole of cheesy mashed potatoes, puffed in the oven until golden brown. The Big Horseradish Twice Baked Potato Pizza contains the best ingredients from the feast. Eating this pizza, whether in Connecticut, Arizona, California, Washington State, or Oregon, brings us together in spirit, with warm memories of Christmas past.

8 to 9 ounces prepared pizza dough at room temperature

1 large Idaho potato

2 tablespoons unsalted butter, softened plus 1 tablespoon melted

¼ to ⅓ cup whole milk, hot

1 tablespoon prepared horseradish, drained

⅛ teaspoon freshly ground black pepper

¼ teaspoon kosher salt, more or less to taste

2 tablespoons chives, chopped – plus additional for garnish

1 tablespoon extra virgin olive oil

1 head Roasted Garlic, Mashed (page 170)

6 ounces Gruyere cheese, shredded and divided

6 to 8 ounces sirloin steak, cooked and sliced ¼ inch thick (see note)

sour cream for garnish

1 Preheat oven to 400° F. Scrub potato and pierce once or twice with a fork. Place directly on oven rack and bake for 55 to 60 minutes or until soft. Remove from oven and cool for about 5 minutes.

2 Cut potato in half lengthwise and remove pulp from skin with a spoon. Place pulp into a medium bowl. Add 2 tablespoons of the butter, ¼ cup hot milk, horseradish, pepper and salt. Mash and stir until potato mixture is smooth. Add remainder of milk if potato mixture is dry. The consistency should resemble that of thick sour cream.

3 Stir in chopped chives. Set mixture aside covered with foil to keep it warm.

4 Roll, stretch and shape dough into a 12 to 14 inch circle or rectangle as per basic directions. Brush dough with a mixture of 1 tablespoon olive oil and 1 tablespoon melted butter.

5 Spread roasted garlic over crust, leaving a ½ inch border and sprinkle with 4 ounces of the Gruyere cheese.

6 Arrange steak slices over top of cheese, dot pizza with spoonsful of the mashed potato mixture, nestling small mounds among the steak. Sprinkle with remaining cheese. If you prefer your steak rare, add it to the pizza during the last 3 to 4 minutes of baking.

7 Bake on a preheated Pizza Grill or on a preheated pizza stone in a 500° F. oven for 10 to 12 minutes or until potatoes are puffed and golden. Rotate pizza after first 4 minutes to prevent sticking.

8 Remove from grill and immediately cut into 8 slices or 12 squares if dough was shaped into a rectangle. Dot each piece with a small dollop of sour cream and sprinkle chopped chives over all.

NOTE: *Bring an 8 to 10 ounce prime strip, rib or sirloin steak about 1½ inch thick to room temperature. Brush with olive oil and season with kosher salt and freshly ground black pepper to taste. Grill over high heat for 4 to 5 minutes per side. Remove steak when it is quite rare as it will cook again on the pizza. Let steak rest 10 to 15 minutes, covered loosely with foil. Slice just before placing on pizza.*

Blazing Maui Kazaui Pizza

Inspired by the fire eaters at a Luau on Kauai, this pizza is an adult version of Mags and Eli's Hawaiian Pizza (Kids' Section.) Layers of sweetness, smokiness and saltiness, interspersed with the soft creamy bite of camembert cheese, this pizza is Polynesian perfection. My initial plan was to ignite the liqueur to finish the pizza with a blazing "Kazaui" but I deemed that too dangerous after a few failed attempts and near incineration of everything in close proximity!

½ cup orange marmalade

1 tablespoon soy sauce

2 fresh cored pineapple rings, ½ inch thick

2 tablespoons walnut or vegetable oil

¼ cup brown sugar

2 tablespoons pineapple liqueur, if desired

4 ounces smoked ham or 4 ounces pancetta in ¼ inch dice

8 to 9 ounces prepared pizza dough at room temperature

2 tablespoons extra virgin olive oil

6 ounces Camembert or Brie cheese, sliced ¼ inch thick, divided

6 Scallions, sliced finely on a sharp angle

Crushed red pepper flakes to taste

1 Stir soy sauce into orange marmalade and set aside.

2 Brush pineapple rings with walnut oil. Place brown sugar on rimmed plate and press each pineapple slice into the sugar to coat. Grill pineapple slices directly on an oiled grill grate over medium-high heat until sugar is slightly caramelized and slices are well marked, about 3 to 4 minutes per side. Remove from grill, cut into small chunks and place in a small bowl. Drizzle with pineapple liqueur (KAZAUI) if desired and set aside for topping.

3 If using pancetta instead of smoked ham, heat a small skillet over medium-high heat, cook pancetta just until fat is rendered; drain on a paper towel lined plate and reserve for topping.

4 Roll, stretch and shape dough into an unrefined rectangular or circular shape approximately 12 to 14 inches according to basic directions. Brush both sides of dough with olive oil and place on a large, rimless baking sheet or pizza peel that has been dusted with cornmeal. Carefully lift dough and lay it on the preheated grill (see Grilled Pizza Primer.) Close grill lid and grill for 3 to 5 minutes or until bottom of crust is golden brown with darker grill marks. Remove from grill with tongs and place grilled side up on a flat baking sheet or pizza peel.

5 Spread marmalade mixture evenly on grilled side of dough to within ½ inch of edge. Space half of the cheese slices evenly over the marmalade.

6 Top with ham or pancetta, drained grilled pineapple, remainder of cheese slices and scallions.

7 Carefully slide pizza onto grill, turning burner directly under pizza to low. Close lid and bake for 5 minutes. Check bottom of crust by lifting the edge with tongs. If it is browning too quickly, turn off burner directly under pizza and continue baking for 5 minutes or until crust is golden and cheese is melted.

8 Remove from heat onto a pizza peel and season with crushed red pepper flakes if desired.

FABULOUS DESSERT: Grill pineapple slices as above, leave whole. Place on a small dessert plate, fill center of slice with a scoop of vanilla frozen yogurt or ice cream, drizzle pineapple liqueur over frozen yogurt or ice cream and sprinkle with toasted coconut flakes.

Tip

Camembert cheese has a bit more of a bite than Brie, but both work equally well on this pizza.

Celi's Calabacitas Pizza

Araceli is a stunning young Mexican woman who I met shortly after moving to Arizona. She is a talented nail technician with whom I have had many conversations about life in Arizona, family, friends and food. Yes, food is a topic that regularly comes up during those wonderful manicures and pedicures. I asked Celi one day what her favorite food is, thinking I would make a pizza for her. "Calabacitas," she said without hesitation; adding that her mother makes "the best" calabacitas. Caramba! Calabacitas on pizza? I asked her to list the ingredients her mother uses, which she willingly did; and then I went to work. The result was "fabuloso". The savory herb crema and Mexican cheese form a heavenly pillow for the calabacitas. This is Mexican comfort food at its best.

8 to 9 ounces prepared pizza dough at room temperature

½ cup Crema with Herbs (recipe follows)

2 tablespoons extra virgin olive oil

1 large yellow onion, sliced or diced

½ jalapeno pepper, seeded and minced

1 small yellow zucchini, cut into small dice

1 small green zucchini, cut into small dice

1 teaspoon fresh oregano leaves

1 ear corn, kernels cut off cob or ½ cup frozen roasted corn kernels, thawed

½ teaspoon kosher salt

¼ teaspoon freshly ground black pepper

2 cloves garlic, minced

4 ounces shredded Asadero cheese, divided. Substitute fontina and/or Monterey Jack.

1 large tomato, diced and drained on paper towels

Cotija or other Mexican hard cheese for grating

1. Heat oil in a heavy 12 inch skillet over medium heat. Add onions and jalapeno pepper and sauté, stirring occasionally until onion is translucent, but not brown; about 5 minutes.
2. Add zucchini and sauté over medium-high heat, stirring occasionally for 5 minutes, or until squash just begins to brown.
3. Add oregano, corn, salt, pepper and garlic. Sauté for 2 to 3 minutes, stirring often. Set this mixture (calabacitas) aside to cool slightly.
4. Spread pizza dough with a thin layer of the crema mixture; sprinkle ½ cup asadero cheese over the crema.
5. Scatter calabacitas over cheese and top with diced tomatoes.
6. Sprinkle remaining asadero over top of pizza.
7. Bake on a preheated Pizza Grill or on a preheated pizza stone in a 500° F. oven, rotating pizza after 4 minutes. Bake for 10 to 12 minutes, or until lightly browned and bubbly.

Immediately grate fresh Cotija cheese over top of pizza. Cut and serve.

Tip

You can substitute 2 Mexican squash in place of the yellow and green zucchini, or use 2 green zucchini if preferred. Total 3 cups diced.

Crema with Herbs – Yield ½ cup

- **3 scallions, white and green parts**
- **6 tablespoons cilantro (½ bunch)**
- **¼ cup sour cream**
- **¼ cup Mexican crema**
- **⅛ teaspoon kosher salt**

1. In a small mixing bowl, blend together sour cream and crema.
2. Slice scallions. Mince scallions and cilantro leaves together
3. Combine minced herbs and the crema mixture and season to taste with salt.

Christmas Eve Pasta Pizza

Our friends Augie and Arlene made this dish together every Christmas Eve. Augie joked that he only knew how to make his part and Arlene knew only hers and that's why they stayed together for more than 50 years. It wasn't until she got sick one year that he learned how to make the dish entirely on his own. Thanks to Augie for sharing their recipe with me – now I can serve it as pizza and experience the warmth and wonder of their love and of the season any time of the year.

- **6 tablespoons extra virgin olive oil, divided; plus extra for finishing**
- **4 large cloves garlic, chopped**
- **1 (2 ounce) can anchovy fillets in oil**
- **¼ cup pine nuts**
- **¼ cup raisins, dark or golden**
- **¼ cup sliced black olives**
- **4 ounces dry angel hair pasta, recommended brand – De Cecco®**
- **8 to 9 ounces prepared pizza dough at room temperature**
- **4 ounces whole milk mozzarella cheese, shredded**
- **1 tablespoon plain dry bread crumbs**
- **1 ounce freshly grated Parmigiano-Reggiano cheese**
- **freshly ground black pepper**
- **fresh flat leaf parsley leaves, chopped**

1 Place water for pasta into a saucepan and turn heat to high. While waiting for water to boil, heat 4 tablespoons of the olive oil in a medium sauté pan over medium-high heat. Add garlic and anchovies with their oil, mashing anchovies with a fork. Cook for 1 minute before adding pine nuts, raisins and olives. Cook and stir until anchovies disintegrate into the oil and garlic is translucent, about 3 minutes. Keep on low heat while pasta cooks.

2 Break pasta strands in half; cook according to package directions to 'al dente' stage. Drain quickly and add to the anchovy sauce. Using tongs, toss to coat pasta. Remove from heat and set aside.

3 Roll, stretch and shape dough into an unrefined 12 by 14 inch rectangular or circular shape according to basic directions. Brush both sides of dough with remaining olive oil and place on a pizza peel or rimless baking sheet that has been dusted with cornmeal. Carefully lift dough and lay it on the preheated grill (see Grilled Pizza Primer.) Close grill lid and grill for 3 to 5 minutes or until bottom of crust is golden brown with darker grill marks. Remove from grill with tongs and place grilled side up on a flat baking sheet or pizza peel dusted with cornmeal.

4 Lightly brush grilled side of crust with some of the oil that is in the sauté pan with the pasta and top with mozzarella. Using tongs, distribute the pasta mixture over the cheese. With a slotted spoon, remove any pine nuts, raisins and olives that remain in the sauté pan and scatter them over the pasta. Sprinkle with bread crumbs and Parmigianno-Reggiano cheese.

5 Carefully slide pizza onto grill, turning burner directly under pizza to low. Close lid and bake for 5 minutes. Check bottom of crust by lifting the edge with tongs. If it is browning too quickly, turn off burner directly under pizza and continue baking for 5 minutes or until crust is golden and cheese is melted.

6 Remove from grill and season with freshly ground black pepper. Drizzle a bit of extra virgin olive oil over pizza and garnish with chopped parsley. Cut and serve.

Chuck's Chicken and Mushroom Tapenade Pizza

One Sunday afternoon, I asked Chuck what he would like for dinner. Without even blinking, he said "pizza." Of course, I thought, what else? I agreed to make him a pizza with the caveat that he choose a topping from ingredients on hand. Since Chuck can eat pizza seven days a week, I knew he would come through. He said, "chicken and mushroom"...that narrowed it down! "Ok," I said, thinking 'BORING' to myself...how ordinary. So, I went to work, combined ingredients I had on hand and Chuck's (blah) Chicken and Mushroom Pizza became Chuck's Chicken and Mushroom Tapenade Pizza. Chuck enjoyed every savory bite.

---

8 to 9 ounces pizza dough at room temperature

8 ounces bulk Italian style chicken sausage, cooked

2 tablespoons extra virgin olive oil, plus extra for drizzling on mushrooms

⅓ cup Marion's Marinara Sauce (page 164)

1 cup Mushroom Tapenade (page 175) use more or less as desired

¾ cup whole milk mozzarella, shredded and divided

4 ounces mushrooms, thickly sliced

shaved Parmigiano-Reggiano cheese

fresh thyme leaves for garnish

1 Heat a 12 inch skillet over medium high heat. Add sausage to skillet and cook, breaking sausage apart as it cooks, for 5 to 8 minutes, or until cooked but not brown. Drain sausage and set aside to cool.

2 Roll stretch and shape the dough into a 12 by 14 inch rectangular shape according to basic directions, and brush with olive oil. Spread ⅓ cup marinara sauce over dough.

3 Evenly distribute 1 cup of the mushroom tapenade over sauce and top with ½ cup mozzarella cheese.

4 Scatter chicken sausage over cheese.

5 Slice mushrooms and drizzle with olive oil. Arrange over pizza and shave fresh Parmigiano-Reggiano cheese over all. (I use a vegetable peeler for shaving cheese.)

6 Bake for 10 minutes on a preheated Pizza Grill or on a preheated pizza stone in a 500° F. oven, rotating after 4 minutes to prevent sticking. Bake until bottom is golden brown and top is bubbly. Remove from grill and immediately sprinkle with fresh thyme. Cut, serve and enjoy.

Desert Heat Pizza

Even though we traveled from Connecticut to Arizona for vacations many times over the years, we were still a little taken back by the desert heat when we moved to Arizona permanently. It was a whole new world; it gets mighty hot here in the summer! Cooking became a bit of a challenge during the height of the summer heat; it was not prudent to turn the oven on, as the air conditioning system was already working overtime and cooking on the stovetop every evening left me with major clean up detail after dinner. So, I began to regularly use the gas grill. There were a few problems with this....monsoons usually occur around dinner time and our patio faced due west so there was no shade to be found. I had to bite the bullet, so to speak, and dance through the raindrops and/or sweat out the heat while grilling. It was that first summer that I perfected my pizza grilling techniques, moving quickly, keeping an eye over the mountains for lightning, and trying not to let the heat get the best of me. To paraphrase Harry S. Truman, 'If you can't stand the heat, get out of the desert!' Not necessary, however, when making this pizza; temper the pizza heat by using a mixture of half jalapeno jack and half Monterey Jack cheese. Enjoy the Desert Heat.

8 (12-15 count) raw shrimp

½ cup Cilantro Pesto, plus 1 tablespoon for marinade (page 173)

1 tablespoon extra virgin olive oil

8 to 9 ounces prepared pizza dough at room temperature

4 ounces pepper jack cheese, shredded

1 ear roasted corn, kernels cut off cob (page 18)

1 small sweet onion such as Vidalia or Maui, halved and cut into thin strips

1 small red or yellow pepper, sliced into thin strips

2 ounces Monterey Jack cheese, shredded

Cotija cheese or other Mexican cheese such as queso fresco, grated

1. Peel and devein shrimp; rinse and pat dry. Cut in half horizontally, then in half crosswise and marinate in a mixture of 1 tablespoon cilantro pesto and 1 tablespoon olive oil. Refrigerate while preparing other ingredients.
2. Roll, stretch and shape dough into a 12 by 14 inch rectangular shape or an irregular circular shape according to basic directions.
3. Spread dough with a thin layer of cilantro pesto, leaving ½ inch border; sprinkle with shredded jalapeno jack cheese or mixture of Monterey Jack and jalapeno jack.
4. Arrange shrimp pieces over cheese and top with roasted corn, onion slices, and pepper strips. Sprinkle Monterey Jack cheese over all.
5. Bake on a preheated Pizza Grill or on a preheated pizza stone in a 500° F. oven for 10 to 12 minutes, or until top is bubbly and bottom of crust is firm and evenly browned, rotating after 4 minutes to prevent sticking.
6. Grate Cotija cheese to taste over pizza immediately after removing from grill/oven.

Tip

For less heat, use a combination of 2 ounces pepper jack cheese and 2 ounces Monterey Jack cheese in step 3.

E's Rockin' Reuben Pizza

Labor Day 2009: My sister Elaine and daughter Jen flew in from WA and CT respectively for a long weekend...a break for each from their demanding careers. There would be no labor on this Labor Day. Floating in the pool in the hot Arizona sun was their therapy. The only decisions to be made involved which SPF sunscreen to use and whether the pool water should be above or below 85 degrees. I waited until they were floating off into a near dream-like state and asked, "If you could have anything you wanted to eat right now, what would it be? "Oh, Linda," Elaine immediately replied, "a roooben". On no labor Labor Day, 2009, an outrageous pizza was created. Not bad for a day's work. What was Jen's favorite food? See Jin Jin's Dilly of a Cheeseburger Pizza!

8 to 9 ounces prepared pizza dough at room temperature

4 teaspoons caraway seeds, divided

2 tablespoons butter

2 tablespoons extra virgin olive oil, additional for brushing crust

1 medium sweet onion such as Vidalia, cut in half and thinly sliced

1 tablespoon coarse mustard

¼ teaspoon freshly ground black pepper

8 ounces sauerkraut in plastic pouch, drained and wrung dry in clean kitchen towel

⅓ cup Russian Dressing (recipe follows) plus extra for finishing

4 ounces whole milk mozzarella, shredded

3 ounces thin slices pastrami or corned beef, cut into 1 inch strips

3 to 4 ounces Swiss cheese, thinly sliced

1. Knead one tablespoon of the caraway seeds into the pizza dough. Shape into a ball, cover and set aside.
2. In a 12 inch skillet, heat oil and butter over medium heat. Add onion and sauté for 15 minutes or until soft and golden brown. Add coarse mustard, black pepper and ½ to 1 teaspoon caraway seeds (the full teaspoon will give you a stronger "rye" flavor.) Stir to combine then add the drained sauerkraut, stir and sauté for 5 minutes longer. Set mixture aside to cool slightly. (This is enough sauerkraut for two pizzas.)
3. Roll, stretch and shape dough into an unrefined 12 to 14 inch circular or rectangular shape according to basic directions, leaving dough a bit thicker around edges. Brush with extra virgin olive oil and spread Russian dressing in an even layer over crust. You may need to use up to ½ cup of dressing depending on size of stretched dough.
4. Sprinkle mozzarella cheese evenly over dressing; then distribute one half of the sauerkraut/onion mixture evenly over cheese.
5. Arrange pastrami or corned beef strips over pizza.
6. Top with slices of Swiss cheese, being careful not to overlap them.
7. Bake on a preheated Pizza Grill or on a preheated pizza stone in a 500° F. oven, rotating pizza after 4 minutes to prevent sticking. Bake for 10 to 12 minutes or until bottom crust is golden and top of pizza is nicely browned and bubbly. After removing pizza from grill, drizzle with additional Russian dressing as desired.

Russian Dressing

- ¾ cup mayonnaise (recommended Hellman's® or Best Foods®)
- 2 tablespoons sour cream
- ¼ cup chili sauce
- 1 tablespoon minced sweet onion such as Vidalia or Maui
- 1 tablespoon minced dill pickle
- 1 teaspoon prepared horseradish
- 1 tablespoon flat leaf parsley, minced
- ¼ teaspoon freshly squeezed lemon juice
- ¼ teaspoon Worcestershire® sauce
- ¼ teaspoon granulated sugar
- ¼ teaspoon kosher salt

1. In a small bowl, combine mayonnaise, sour cream and chili sauce; stir until smooth.
2. Add remaining ingredients and stir to combine.
3. Refrigerate in a sealed container until ready to use. This dressing will keep for up to one week in the refrigerator.

NOTE: *This recipe makes enough dressing for one pizza with plenty left over to dress an amazing salad. Try roughly shredded, crisp iceberg lettuce, coarsely chopped, cooked red beets and thinly sliced sweet onion; add some chick peas for a complete lunch or dinner salad.*

Fabulous Fortieth Anniversary Pizza

On December 27th, my husband and I celebrated our 40th wedding anniversary at a formal dinner in Connecticut among cherished friends and family members. Festive decorations captured the essence of the holidays – from flickering candles to fancy floral arrangements, our daughter fastidiously planned and executed every detail, leaving nothing to chance. No, we did not have pizza that evening; rather my inspiration came from one of the most unusual gifts we received – a "Lobster Gram". How fortuitous, I thought...I can commemorate the evening by creating a pizza that incorporates our favorite food – lobster. My plan is to make this pizza every year on our anniversary and recall the love we felt that evening from those we hold most dear.

4 tablespoons extra virgin olive oil, divided

4 tablespoons unsalted butter

1 large shallot, peeled and thinly sliced (approximately 3 ounces)

2 cloves garlic, chopped

⅛ teaspoon crushed red pepper flakes

8 to 9 ounces prepared pizza dough at room temperature

6 to 8 ounces Manchego cheese, shredded

6 to 8 ounces lobster meat, cut into chunks and cooked in butter

2 tablespoons fresh chives, thinly sliced

sea salt and freshly ground pepper

1 lemon, freshly grated zest; squeeze of juice for finishing

Tip

Add more or less cheese and/or lobster meat as desired. I use one 8 ounce lobster tail which I cut into chunks and sauté for 2 minutes in 2 tablespoons of unsalted butter.

1 Heat 2 tablespoons of the oil in a medium sauté pan over medium heat. Add butter and heat until butter foams; add shallots, stir and sauté for 2 to 3 minutes or until translucent and just beginning to brown. Add chopped garlic and crushed red pepper flakes, stir and cook 1 minute longer until garlic is lightly browned. Do not let garlic burn as it will taste bitter. Remove pan from heat and using a slotted spoon, remove shallots from butter sauce; set aside to cool. Reserve sauce for topping.

2 Roll, stretch and shape dough into a 12 by 14 inch unrefined rectangular or circular shape according to basic directions. Brush both sides of dough with remaining two tablespoons of the olive oil. Place on a large, rimless baking sheet or pizza peel dusted with cornmeal. Carefully lift dough and lay it on the preheated grill (see Grilled Pizza Primer.) Close grill lid and grill for 3 to 5 minutes or until bottom of crust is golden brown with darker grill marks. Remove from grill with tongs and place grilled side up on a flat baking sheet or pizza peel dusted with cornmeal.

3 Spread grilled side of dough with butter sauce in which the shallots were cooked, using a pastry brush to distribute sauce and garlic bits. Sprinkle half the cheese evenly over the dough.

4 Arrange lobster meat over the cheese, top with sautéed shallots and remainder of the cheese.

5 Carefully slide pizza onto grill, turning burner directly under pizza to low. Close lid and bake for 5 minutes. Check bottom of crust by lifting the edge with tongs. If it is browning too quickly, turn off burner directly under pizza and continue baking for 5 minutes or until crust is golden and cheese is melted.

6 Remove from grill and sprinkle with fresh chives; season with sea salt and freshly ground black pepper to taste. Using a Microplane®, grate lemon zest over all then squeeze a bit of the fresh lemon juice over top of pizza as desired. Cut and serve immediately. Smile, it's a celebration!

Fully 'Dressed' Pizza

Thanksgiving dinner always brought on the 'heated discussions' in our house. One topic that would not go away over the years was about what to put into a good turkey dressing. My mother loved lots of apples and onions, I loved Italian sausage (which my mother always picked out as she ate,) and my sister Elaine insisted there be plenty of mushrooms and roasted chestnuts. It got worse, should it be baked in the bird or in a casserole? We went on and on and on. We could never agree on the perfect dressing and eventually learned to manage the holiday by allowing the person stuffing the bird to choose what went into the dressing; and unless you wanted to say how absolutely wonderful that dressing was, you didn't comment. This pizza is topped with a combination of everything my family members loved in their turkey dressing – the 'people pleaser' in me lives on!

8 to 12 ounces sweet Italian sausage, bulk or links with casings removed

2 tablespoons unsalted butter

1 small yellow onion, finely chopped

1 small Granny Smith apple, cored and cut into small dice

1 to 2 teaspoons fresh thyme leaves

1 to 2 teaspoons fresh sage leaves, chopped, plus a few whole leaves for garnish

1 teaspoon kosher salt

½ teaspoon freshly ground black pepper

3 cloves garlic, minced

6 ounces baby portabella mushrooms, cleaned and quartered

½ cup dry white wine like Sauvignon Blanc

1 cup herb seasoned stuffing cubes, dry

1 cup chestnuts, roasted, peeled and sliced (or jarred)

1 tablespoon fresh flat leaf parsley, chopped

8 to 9 ounces prepared pizza dough at room temperature

2 tablespoons extra virgin olive oil

4 ounces Gruyere cheese, shredded and divided

½ cup whole berry cranberry sauce (or to taste)

½ cup hot turkey gravy (optional)

1 Heat a large 14 inch skillet or 5 quart sauté pan over medium-high heat. Add sausage and cook for about 7 minutes, breaking it apart and stirring as it cooks. Remove sausage and set aside to cool. Melt butter in the same pan over medium heat; add onions and diced apple and sauté for 8 minutes. Add chopped thyme, chopped sage, salt and pepper and stir to combine. Raise heat to medium-high and stir in garlic and mushrooms. Cook 10 minutes longer, stirring occasionally.

2 Stir in wine, scraping up any bits remaining on bottom of the pan. Add sausage, stuffing cubes, chestnuts and chopped parsley to the mixture in the pan. Toss gently, allowing stuffing cubes to absorb moisture from vegetables. Cover and set aside for topping.

3 Roll, stretch and shape dough into a 12 to 14 inch unrefined circular or rectangular shape according to basic directions. Brush dough with olive oil. Scatter ¾ of the Gruyere cheese over the dough. Distribute enough of the 'stuffing' mixture to evenly and lightly cover the cheese layer, leaving a ½ inch border. Sprinkle remaining Gruyere cheese over all.

4 Bake on a preheated pizza grill or on a preheated pizza stone in a 500° F. oven, rotating after 4 minutes to prevent sticking. Bake for 10 to 12 minutes or until the crust is golden and firm and top is bubbly and nicely browned.

5 Remove from the heat, drizzle with hot gravy if using, dot top of pizza with spoonsful of cold cranberry sauce and garnish with whole sage leaves.

Cut and serve immediately.

NOTE: *Serve your Thanksgiving feast with a glass of cool, crisp Sauvignon Blanc.*

Gary's Cheesy Chili Fries Pizza

Cheesy Chili Fries Pizza, the junk food junkie's dream! Named for one of our dear friends Gary who has been blessed with the metabolism of a world class athlete, this pizza is loaded with spicy chili and crispy fries, hidden under a layer of melted Mexican cheese. Is it over the top? Of course, but that never stopped a true junk food junkie – go for it!

- **1½ cups Basic Beef and Beans Chili, divided (page 105)**
- **8 ounces frozen crispy potato fries**
- **8 to 9 ounces prepared pizza dough at room temperature**
- **2 tablespoons extra virgin olive oil**
- **4 ounces shredded 4 cheese Mexican blend, divided. Extra for topping if desired.**
- **½ cup shredded asadero or jack cheese**
- **crushed red pepper flakes**
- **Tabasco Sauce®**

1. Prepare Basic Beef Chili (page 105) and set aside to cool.
2. Pre-bake fries according to package directions, removing from oven 3 to 5 minutes before recommended end of baking time. Set aside for topping.
3. Roll, stretch and shape dough into an unrefined 12 to 14 inch circular shape as per basic directions. Brush dough with olive oil and cover with ¾ cup Mexican cheese blend.
4. Spoon one cup of the room temperature chili over the cheese layer and top with a layer of pre-cooked fries. Spoon remainder of the chili over the fries and sprinkle the remaining Mexican cheese and the asadero cheese over all.
5. Bake on a preheated Pizza Grill or on a preheated pizza stone in a 500° F. oven for 10 to 12 minutes, rotating pizza after 4 minutes to prevent sticking. Bake until crust is firm and golden, chili is bubbling and cheese is melted.
6. Remove from heat and immediately top with additional Mexican blend cheese as desired. Sprinkle with crushed red pepper flakes or a few shakes of Tabasco Sauce® to taste. Cut and serve.

Tip

If you plan to use the chili for a pizza topping, you can eliminate the beans.

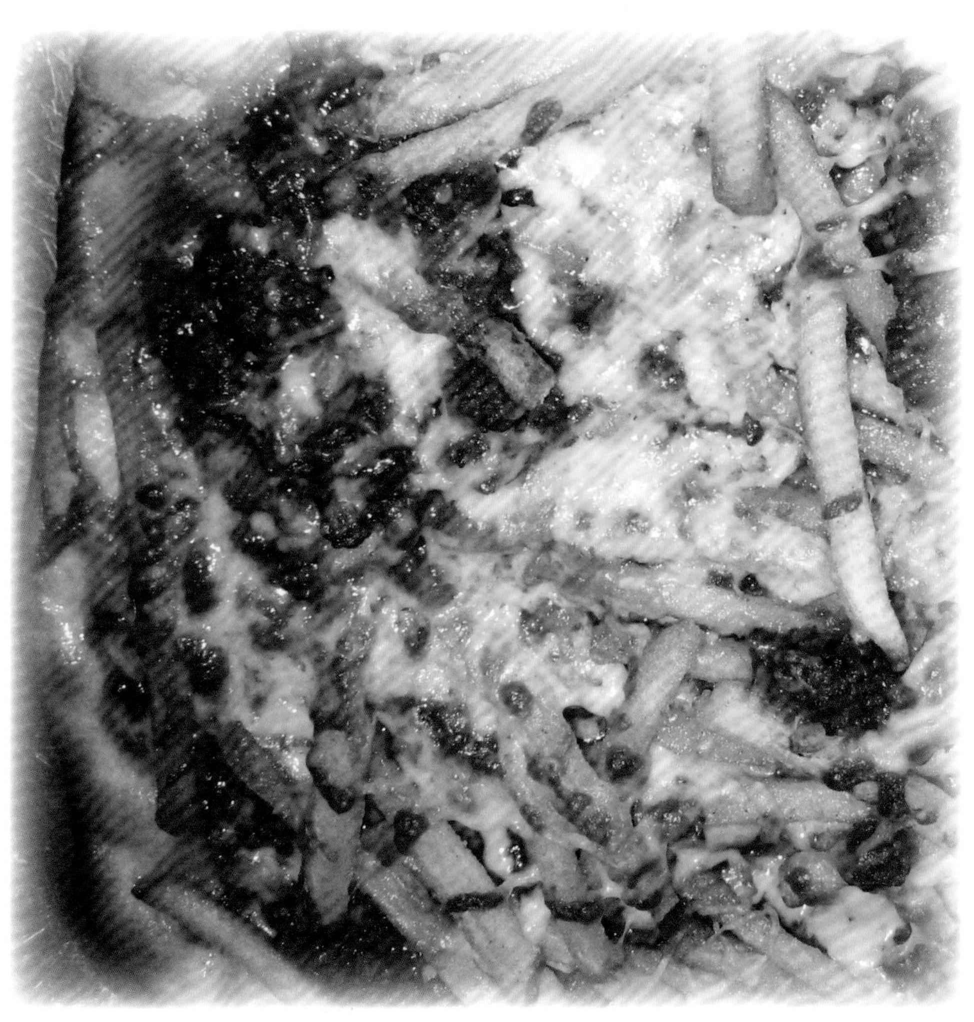

Janos Gone 'Wild'er Pizza

Janos Gone 'Wild'er Pizza

Janos Wilder is a nationally acclaimed chef, winner of the James Beard Foundation: Top Chef in the Southwest 2000 and Top Chef Southwest Nominee 1992 – 1999. Currently, Chef Wilder is a 2012 James Beard Semi-finalist for Outstanding Chef: United States. He has also received other honors and awards too numerous to list. Imagine how thrilled I was to learn that this extraordinarily successful restaurateur in Tucson, Arizona would be teaching ***me*** *the secrets of The Southwest Pantry. Yes, my thoughtful husband had done it again, arranged for me to attend two of Janos' wonderfully informative, highly entertaining cooking classes. Chef Janos' detailed instructions and demonstration of various techniques were invaluable in helping me to better understand and expand my southwest cooking repertoire. Tantalizing aromas filled the air as Chef Janos diced garden tomatoes, onions and roasted chilies for the salsa fresca, toasted pepitas, and pureed poblanos for the crema sauce, all the while relating humorous stories of his travels and culinary experiences.*

Although he didn't realize it at the time, Chef Janos inspired me to create this extraordinary pizza during his class. The idea came to mind as Chef described a use for the Smoked Poblano Crema he had just prepared. Chef Janos talked of constructing a quesadilla using some of the smoked poblano crema, grilled mushroom slices with garlic, roasted chilies and Manchego cheese. "The crema gets warm and the cheese gets gooey...you will be so happy," he said with such passion and animation, the sighs were audible as every student in his class longed for just one bite of that glorious quesadilla. Chef Janos' idea for a fabulously gooey quesadilla makes for one 'Wild'ly delicious pizza. Thanks, Chef Janos Wilder!

- **1 recipe Smoked Poblano Crema (recipe follows)**
- **6 tablespoons extra virgin olive oil, divided**
- **3 large cloves garlic**
- **1 roasted poblano chili, peeled, seeded and cut into ½ inch strips**
- **2 large portobella mushroom caps, brushed clean and cut into ½ inch thick slices**
- **9 ounces prepared pizza dough at room temperature**
- **6 ounces Manchego cheese, shredded**
- **1 small serrano chili, seeded and minced**
- **kosher salt and freshly ground black pepper to taste**
- **freshly grated lime zest and fresh lime juice to taste**
- **2 tablespoons pepitas, lightly toasted in a bit of oil and salted**

1. Warm 4 tablespoons of the oil in a small skillet. Peel and smash garlic and add to oil. Barely simmer for 5 minutes, or until garlic just begins to brown. Remove from heat and set aside to cool slightly.

2. Brush mushroom slices with reserved garlic oil. Season lightly with kosher salt and freshly ground black pepper. Grill over medium-high heat for 3 to 4 minutes per side, or until mushrooms are slightly softened and have nice grill marks. Remove from grill and set aside to cool slightly for topping.

3. Roll, stretch and shape dough into an unrefined 10 by 12 inch rectangular or circular shape according to basic directions. Brush both sides of dough with the olive oil and place on a large, rimless baking sheet or pizza peel that has been dusted with cornmeal. Carefully lift dough and lay it on the preheated grill, turning burner under dough to low. (See Grilled Pizza Primer.) Close grill lid and grill for 3 to 5 minutes or until bottom of crust is golden brown with darker grill marks. Remove from grill with tongs and place grilled side up on a flat baking sheet or pizza peel that has been lightly dusted with cornmeal.

4. Spread just enough of the Smoked Poblano Crema over the grilled side of the dough to coat evenly, about ½ cup. Reserve remaining crema for finishing. Sprinkle half the Manchego cheese over the crema.

5 Arrange grilled mushroom slices, strips of roasted chili and minced serrano chili over cheese. Top with remaining Manchego cheese.

6 Carefully slide pizza onto grill, turning burner directly under pizza to low. Close lid and bake for 5 minutes. Check bottom of crust by lifting the edge with tongs. If it is browning too quickly, turn off burner directly under pizza and continue baking for 5 minutes or until crust is golden and cheese is melted.

7 Remove from heat; season with salt and pepper. Spoon small dollops of the remaining poblano crema over pizza; top with freshly grated lime zest and a squeeze of lime juice. Scatter toasted pepitas over all. Cut and serve immediately.

TO ROAST CHILIS: Preheat a grill or broiler to high. Brush olive oil on whole poblano peppers and season with kosher salt and freshly ground black pepper. Place on grate of grill or on a broiler pan so peppers are 2 inches from heating element. Blacken peppers for about 10 to 15 minutes, turning often. Once skins are almost completely blackened and blistered, remove peppers from heat. Place peppers into a brown paper bag on a plate and fold top of bag to seal or place peppers in a bowl and seal with plastic wrap for about 10 minutes or until peppers have had a chance to sweat and soften a bit more. Remove from bag or bowl and peel off skin with your fingers...messy, but worth the effort! Do not be tempted to do this under running water as you will wash away much of the wonderful flavor. Cut off top and base of each pepper and slice it open. Scrape off membranes and seeds with a knife. Cut into strips and set aside for topping.

Chef Janos Wilder's Smoked Poblano Crema - Yield 1 cup

2 smoked poblano chilis

1 cup sour cream

kosher salt

freshly ground black pepper

1 Cut off top and base of each smoked pepper and slice it open. Scrape off membranes and seeds with a knife; cut into strips. Once cooled, place peppers into a food processor fitted with a metal blade; pulse 3 or 4 times to puree.

2 Add sour cream to pureed peppers and process until completely combined; season to taste with kosher salt and pepper.

SMOKED CHILIS: Soak 1 cup mesquite chips in water for about 20 to 30 minutes. Prepare a charcoal fire or preheat a gas grill. Drain mesquite chips; scatter over hot coals or place in a smoker box if using a gas grill. Oil chilies, place on grill grate over low heat, cover grill and smoke for 20 to 25 minutes.

Jenny Loves Tacos Pizza

Jenny always had a deep and abiding love for tacos. Given a choice, she would choose tacos over any other food and argued it was suitable for any occasion from celebrating straight 'A's on yet another report card to choosing a theme for her next birthday party. Most kids brought cupcakes to school on their birthday to share with classmates; not Jenny, she brought tacos. Jenny is now all grown up and friends and colleagues know her only as Jennifer or Attorney Groves, but there is a piece of little Jenny who is still very much alive and she confessed to me quite recently that she still loved tacos and could probably eat fifty if given the chance.

Taco Seasoning Mix (recipe follows)

1 pound ground beef, 80% lean

½ cup water

½ cup tomato sauce, divided – recommended brand – Hunt's®

8 to 9 ounces prepared pizza dough at room temperature

4 ounces shredded cheddar cheese, or smoked cheddar cheese

6 scallions, white and green parts thinly sliced

4 ounces Monterey Jack or jalapeno jack cheese, shredded

1 small sweet white onion, minced

½ cup black olives, sliced

1 large, ripe tomato, seeded and finely chopped

sour cream

taco sauce

shredded iceberg lettuce

1. Prepare taco seasoning mix and set aside.
2. Heat a 12inch skillet, over medium-high heat. Add beef and cook, breaking apart with a wooden spoon, until beef is cooked and lightly browned, about 5 to 7 minutes. Drain fat from beef mixture. Add water, ¼ cup of the tomato sauce and Taco Seasoning Mix, stir to combine. Reduce heat to medium-low and simmer partially covered for 5 minutes, stirring occasionally. Remove lid and simmer 5 minutes longer or until most of liquid is absorbed. Set aside to cool.
3. Roll, stretch and shape dough into an unrefined circular or rectangular shape approximately 12 to 14 inches according to basic directions. Spread ¼ cup tomato sauce on the dough then sprinkle with the cheddar cheese leaving a border of approximately ½ inch.
4. Spread cooled taco filling over cheese – I recommend that you use only one half of the mixture, but feel free to load it up if you so desire. Be sure to allow extra baking time if you use more than one half of the beef mixture.
5. Top with scallions and Monterey Jack cheese.
6. Bake on a preheated Pizza Grill or on a preheated pizza stone in a 500° F. oven, rotating pizza after 4 minutes to prevent sticking. Bake for 10 to 12 minutes or until crust is firm and golden and topping is bubbly. You may need to bake for an additional few minutes if you used all the beef taco mixture; and you will **definitely** need to use a fork and knife to eat your pizza once you add the taco toppings to your slice.
7. Remove from the heat and cut into squares or wedges. Set out taco sauce. Place onion, olives, tomato, sour cream and lettuce in small bowls. Allow each person to top his or her own taco pizza piece with toppings of his/her own choice. As Jenny would say, 'this is a very personal matter.'

Taco Seasoning Mix

- **2 teaspoons instant minced onion (dehydrated minced onion)**
- **½ teaspoon instant minced garlic (dehydrated garlic flakes)**
- **1 teaspoon kosher salt**
- **1 teaspoon chili powder**
- **½ teaspoon cornstarch**
- **½ teaspoon crushed dried red pepper flakes**
- **¼ teaspoon Mexican oregano (crushed)**
- **½ teaspoon ground cumin**

1 Combine all ingredients in a small bowl and spoon mixture into a small airtight container. Mixture can be stored in a cool, dry place for up to 6 months.

Tip

You can use the heated leftover taco mix and the condiments for a tasty "Taco Salad".

Jin Jin's Dilly of a Cheeseburger Pizza

Jin Jin loves the taste of a juicy, cheese-oozing, fully loaded cheeseburger. But her figure friendly conscience says "don't you dare!" Try a slice of Jin Jin's pizza for a taste of the forbidden without the all the guilt. Okay, without as much guilt.

8 to 9 ounces prepared pizza dough at room temperature

12 ounces 80% lean ground beef

2 teaspoons vegetable oil

¾ teaspoon Worcestershire® sauce

½ teaspoon salt – or to taste

½ teaspoon pepper – or to taste

½ teaspoon dry mustard

⅓ cup tomato sauce – recommended brand - Hunt's®

2 tomatoes, sliced approximately ⅛ inch thick

½ sweet onion such as Vidalia or Maui, cut into thin strips

4 to 6 ounces Havarti cheese with dill, shredded – recommended brand – Boar's Head®

½ cup sweet onion, finely diced – for finishing

½ cup dill pickles, finely diced – for finishing

1. In a 12 inch skillet, heat 2 teaspoons oil over medium high heat. Add beef to skillet and brown, breaking it apart as it cooks. Stir in dry mustard, salt, pepper and Worcestershire® sauce. Continue cooking for 5 to 8 minutes, or until cooked, but not browned. Allow beef mixture to sit in its own juice as it cools slightly.
2. Spread tomato sauce on dough. Sprinkle with ¾ of the cheese. Top with drained ground beef mixture. Arrange tomato and onion slices over beef. Sprinkle with remainder of cheese.
3. Bake on a preheated Pizza Grill or on a pizza stone in a 500° F. oven 10 to 12 minutes, or until lightly browned. Rotate pizza after first 4 minutes to be sure it is not sticking.
4. Remove from heat and immediately sprinkle with diced sweet onion and dill pickles. Use more or less as desired.

John's 'Just Pizza' Pizza

John loves the simple things in life...sipping a cup of coffee on the dock as the sun rises, fishing, and hanging out with his wife Karen, family and good friends on the Indian River in Florida. As you might guess, John also loves simple foods; his favorite food – Italian food! When asked what kind of pizza he likes, John said "just pizza." He went on, "you know the kind loaded with sauce and sausage and meatballs and thick cheese." Then he tipped his head back and raised an imaginary slice of pizza to his mouth while describing the awesomeness of biting into that slice and pulling all the hot, stringy cheese into his mouth. How could I not make this amazingly simple pizza in his honor?

3 tablespoons extra virgin olive oil, divided

8 ounces bulk sweet Italian sausage

9 to 10 ounces prepared pizza dough at room temperature

1 cup Marion's Marinara Sauce, divided (page 164). Alternatively, use good quality jarred sauce.

½ cup shredded whole milk mozzarella

4 to 6 cooked Italian meatballs, sliced ¼ inch thick (page 171)

8 ounces fresh whole milk mozzarella, sliced ¼ inch thick (approximately 8 slices)

¼ cup freshly grated Parmigiano-Reggiano cheese, plus additional for finishing

extra heated marinara sauce for dipping, if desired

1. Heat 1 tablespoon olive oil in a medium sauté pan over medium-high heat. Add sausage and cook for 3 to 5 minutes, breaking it apart as it cooks. Sausage should be cooked, but not browned. Drain and discard oil from sausage; set aside to cool. Eliminate olive oil if using a non-stick pan.

2. Roll, stretch and shape dough into a 12 to 14 inch unrefined circular shape according to basic directions. Brush dough with remaining 2 tablespoons olive oil. Spread ½ cup marinara sauce over dough and sprinkle the shredded mozzarella cheese evenly over the sauce.

3. Scatter cooked sausage over the cheese. Slice meatballs and layer over sausage.

4. Arrange slices of mozzarella over the pizza and spoon remaining sauce over the cheese slices. Sprinkle Parmigiano-Reggiano over all.

5. Bake on a preheated Pizza Grill or on a preheated pizza stone in a 500° F. oven, rotating after 4 minutes to prevent sticking. Bake for 10 to 12 minutes or until bottom of crust is firm and golden brown, top is bubbly and cheese is lightly browned.

6. Remove from grill or oven and grate Parmigiano-Reggiano over pizza as desired. Cut and serve immediately with extra hot marinara sauce for dipping or drizzling.

Judi's Veal 'Parmelone' Pizza

One beautiful, cool and breezy Arizona afternoon, my wonderful friend Judi and I sat outside taking in the beauty of the mountains and reminiscing about our childhoods...or should I say, about favorite foods associated with our childhoods? Judi spoke of her Belgian grandfather and her Italian grandmother, a marriage made in heaven – as far as food goes! Gramps made amazing Wiener Schnitzel and, when paired with grandma Angelina's fresh crusty Italian bread, homemade sauce and provolone cheese, that schnitzel became the centerpiece of Judi's favorite childhood food. Yes, Gramps made Judi sandwiches that you could almost taste as she lovingly described them today. On Judi's Veal 'Parmolone' Pizza, the flavors of Veal Parmesan and Gramp's Wiener Schnitzel Provolone sandwich of days gone by are beautifully married!

2 Breaded Veal Cutlets (recipe follows), cut into ½ inch wide strips

9 ounces prepared pizza dough at room temperature

2 tablespoons extra virgin olive oil

1 cup Marion's Marinara Sauce, divided (page 164)

4 to 6 ounce ball whole milk mozzarella cheese, sliced ⅛ inch thick

2 to 4 ounces provolone cheese, thin deli slices

1 teaspoon lemon zest, finely grated on a Microplane®

crushed red pepper flakes, to taste

Parmigiano-Reggiano cheese for finishing

1 Roll, stretch and shape dough into an unrefined circular shape approximately 12 to 14 inches according to basic directions. Brush crust with olive oil and spread ½ cup marinara sauce evenly over dough.

2 Arrange mozzarella slices over sauce; place strips of breaded veal over all.

3 Place provolone cheese over top of veal and dot top of entire pizza with small spoonsful of remaining marinara.

4 Bake on a preheated Pizza Grill or on a preheated pizza stone in a 500° F. oven, rotating pizza after 4 minutes to prevent sticking. Bake for 10 minutes or until crust is firm and golden and cheese and sauce are bubbling.

5 Remove from heat and sprinkle lemon zest and, if desired, crushed red pepper flakes over pizza. Grate Parmigiano-Reggiano cheese over all. Cut and serve immediately.

Tip

Using higher amounts of cheese will produce a gooey pizza that will resemble a hot veal parmesan grinder. Two to three minutes additional cooking time may be needed, but it is so worth it.

Breaded Veal Cutlets - Yield 2

- **2 veal cutlets (scaloppini) approximately 2 to 3 ounces each – pounded thin. See cook's note.**
- **½ cup all-purpose flour for dredging**
- **½ teaspoon kosher salt, divided**
- **½ teaspoon freshly ground black pepper, divided**
- **1 egg, slightly beaten**
- **1 tablespoon water**
- **½ cup Panko, Japanese breadcrumbs**
- **2 tablespoons Parmigiano-Reggiano cheese, freshly grated**
- **½ teaspoon Italian seasoning**
- **canola or other vegetable oil for frying (Gramps preferred clarified LARD!)**

1 In a shallow bowl or on a rimmed plate, mix flour with ¼ teaspoon each salt and pepper. Mix water into beaten egg in another shallow bowl; stir the Parmigiano-Reggiano cheese, Italian seasoning, and remainder of salt and pepper into the Panko on another rimmed plate.

2 To bread the veal, dredge one cutlet in flour mixture, shake off excess, then dip into the egg, allowing excess to drip off. Press into bread crumbs to coat meat evenly. Place on a baking sheet and repeat with remaining cutlet(s). At this point, cutlets can be covered and refrigerated for up to two hours.

3 Pour oil into a medium, heavy bottom sauté pan to the depth of approximately ½ inch. Heat oil until a small piece of the Panko sizzles and browns quickly when dropped into the pan. Depending on the size of the pan, carefully place one or both cutlets into the pan. Cutlets should not overlap. Cook for approximately 1½ to 2 minutes on the first side. Turn the cutlet and brown for 1 to 2 minutes longer to crisp the breading on the second side. Remove from oil, place on a paper towel lined plate and loosely cover with foil to keep warm for topping.

COOK'S NOTE: *Depending on the size of the cutlet, you might choose to cut each cutlet in half before breading.*

Karen's Lobster Mac Pizza

This amazingly decadent pizza is topped with baked macaroni and cheese that is loaded with lobster. My inspiration – my dear friend Karen Quoka's creamy lobster macaroni and cheese casserole that, for me, was the highlight of her Christmas Eve party every year. Even though her table was laden from end to end with fabulous appetizers, entrées and delicate confections, I would always find myself standing near the mac and cheese casserole so it would not be obvious that I was deftly slipping serving after serving onto my plate. Pure heaven!

- **1 recipe Provolone Cheese Sauce, divided (page 168)**
- **1 tablespoon unsalted butter**
- **¼ cup Panko bread crumbs**
- **4 ounces dry cavatappi pasta or ridged elbows**
- **8 ounces cooked lobster meat, cut into chunks**
- **1 tablespoon fresh thyme leaves, chopped plus whole leaves for garnish**
- **9 ounces prepared pizza dough at room temperature**
- **white truffle oil to taste**

1. In a small skillet, melt butter over medium-high heat. When foam subsides, sauté Panko breadcrumbs in butter until light golden. Set aside for topping.

2. Cook cavatappi to 'al dente' according to package directions. Drain and place in a medium mixing bowl. Set aside ½ cup of the Provolone Cheese Sauce and add enough of the remaining sauce to completely coat the pasta. Stir to combine then fold in the lobster. Cover to keep warm for topping.

3. Knead thyme leaves into prepared pizza dough. Roll, stretch and shape dough into an unrefined 12 to 14 inch rectangular or circular shape according to basic directions. Spread one half cup of the provolone sauce in an even layer over the dough. Bake on a preheated Pizza Grill or on a preheated pizza stone in a 500° F. oven for 4 minutes. Remove to a pizza peel or rimless baking sheet that has been lightly dusted with cornmeal and immediately close grill lid or oven door to retain the heat.

4. Spread macaroni, cheese and lobster mixture on the partially baked pizza dough. Top with buttered Panko crumbs. Return to Pizza Grill or oven and bake for 8 to 10 minutes longer or until crust is firm and golden and topping is bubbly and lightly browned.

5. Remove from heat and drizzle with white truffle oil to taste; sprinkle with one tablespoon whole thyme leaves. Cut and serve immediately.

Tip

You can take this pizza over the top by garnishing it with a shaved white or black truffle.

The interesting thing about this pizza is that it is like eating a piping hot bowl of lobster macaroni and cheese with your hands – no bowl or fork required; just a perfect crust in which to cradle that gooey goodness. It is beyond heavenly.

Kim's Caramelized Onion and Bacon Pizza

One of my daughter-in-law Kim's favorite foods is far from pretentious; it is onion and bacon pizza. She loves the down-to-earth flavor combination. I took this to a new level when creating her pizza by using onions that I slowly caramelized in bacon fat – never a bad thing - and by adding a layer of mushroom tapenade as a base for this pizza. The result is an amazingly complex flavor that keeps you saying, "just one more slice!"

8 to 9 ounces prepared pizza dough at room temperature

2 tablespoons extra virgin olive oil

1 cup Mushroom Tapenade (page 175)

6 ounces shredded whole milk mozzarella cheese (approximately ¾ cup)

1 cup Basic Bacon Caramelized Onions (page 169)

diced bacon from recipe (4 ounces)

¼ cup freshly grated Parmigiano-Reggiano cheese, plus extra for garnish

1. Roll, stretch and shape dough into an unrefined 12 by 14 inch rectangular or circular shape according to basic directions. Brush dough with olive oil.
2. Spread dough with the Mushroom Tapenade, being careful to distribute it evenly up to ½ inch from edge.
3. Sprinkle mozzarella cheese over mushrooms and top with caramelized onions and diced bacon.
4. Top entire pizza with Parmigiano-Reggiano.
5. Bake on a preheated Pizza Grill or on a preheated pizza stone in a 500° F. oven for 10 minutes, rotating pizza after first 4 minutes to prevent sticking. Bake until bottom crust is firm and golden and cheese is bubbling.
6. Remove from grill, grate additional Parmigiano-Reggiano over pizza, cut and serve immediately.

GRILLING DIRECTIONS:

1. Stretch dough into a large, somewhat rectangular shape about 12 by 14 inches.
2. Brush both sides of dough with oil and place on a large, rimless baking sheet or pizza peel that has been lightly dusted with cornmeal. Carefully lift dough and lay it on the pre-heated grill (see Grilled Pizza Primer.) Close grill lid and grill for 3 to 5 minutes or until bottom of crust is golden brown with darker grill marks. Remove from grill with tongs and place grilled side up on a flat baking sheet or pizza peel.
3. Continue with steps 2, 3, and 4 in directions above.
4. Carefully slide pizza onto grill, turning burner directly under pizza to low. Close lid and bake for 5 minutes. Check bottom of crust by lifting the edge with tongs. If it is browning too quickly, turn off burner under pizza and continue baking for 4 to 5 minutes longer or until crust is golden and top is bubbly.
5. Using tongs, carefully slide pizza from grill onto pizza peel or flat cookie sheet. Grate additional fresh Parmigiano-Reggiano over hot pizza, cut and serve immediately.

Lin's Labor of Love Lasagne Pizza

During my childhood, holiday dinners at our house were always somewhat chaotic. We were a family of six so the kitchen table was quite crowded already, and with company added to the mix, things became really tight. Before Thanksgiving dinner, my father would go into the cellar and bring up 'the board' while my sister and I set the table. Then the arguments about who had to sit on the dreaded board began. This narrow board was placed on two chairs, bridging the space between to create and extra 'chair' for the loser. The second of four girls, I was a shy and skinny kid, quite invisible at times. As you might guess, I was always the loser who sat on the board through those special dinners, feet dangling, being ever so careful not to lean backwards. There was only one extra chair in the house that would fit at the table, a little antique ice cream parlor chair with a poorly padded seat; that was my mother's chair since most of her time was spent running back and forth serving people and, for her, comfort was not an issue.

The traditional Thanksgiving meal at the Sorrentino house never varied; it began with individual antipasto plates, then turkey soup, followed by a huge pan of my mother's homemade lasagna. She worked for days preparing all the ingredients, from the perfectly seasoned meatballs to the fresh crepes that she used in place of packaged lasagna noodles, and every year she would call my Aunt Lena to ask her the exact same question, "What goes on the top layer?" By the time we finished the first three courses, no one really wanted the turkey with all the trimmings. Most years, the turkey was put on hold for a few hours while we lazed around, too full and tired to do much more than watch our tiny TV. This pizza is a tribute to my mother's labor intensive lasagna which was only prepared twice a year. Since I love to cook and have time, I use freshly made dough, home made marinara sauce and freshly baked meatballs for my pizza. You, however, can cut the labor and keep the love by using purchased dough, sauce and meatballs with equally delicious results.

---

2 tablespoons extra virgin olive oil

2 cloves garlic

2 sweet Italian sausages

2 to 3 Italian Meatballs (page 171)

1½ cups mozzarella cheese, shredded and divided

¾ cup whole milk ricotta cheese

2 tablespoons fresh flat parsley leaves, chopped

2 tablespoons Parmigiano-Reggiano cheese, grated; plus extra for finishing

½ teaspoon kosher salt

⅛ teaspoon freshly ground black pepper

8 to 9 ounces prepared pizza dough at room temperature

¾ cup Marion's Marinara Sauce divided plus additional sauce for finishing (page 164)

1. Warm oil in a small skillet. Peel and smash garlic and add to oil. Barely simmer for 5 minutes, or until garlic just begins to brown. Remove from heat and set aside

2. Heat a 10 inch skillet over medium-high heat. Remove sausage from casing and cook for 5 minutes, breaking apart and stirring as it cooks. Drain oil from sausage and cool slightly. Slice cooked meatballs and set aside for topping.

3. In a small bowl, combine ½ cup mozzarella, ricotta, chopped parsley, 2 tablespoons grated Parmigiano cheese, salt and pepper.

4. Roll, stretch and shape dough into an unrefined 12 by 14 inch rectangular or circular shape according to basic directions. Brush dough with garlic oil. Spread ½ cup marinara sauce evenly over dough.

5 Sprinkle ½ cup mozzarella cheese over sauce. Arrange sliced meatballs over cheese then scatter cooked sausage over all.

6 Dot top of pizza with small spoonsful of ricotta mixture. Sprinkle remaining ½ cup mozzarella over pizza and drizzle with ¼ cup marinara sauce. Grate additional Parmigianino-Reggiano cheese over all if desired.

7 Bake on a preheated Pizza Grill or preheated pizza stone in a 500° F. oven, rotating pizza after 4 minutes to prevent sticking. Bake for 10 to 12 minutes or until crust is firm and golden and cheese is bubbly. Remove from heat; cut and serve with additional sauce to taste.

To this day, when a bunch of us get together we all have a good laugh when someone says, "Get the board!"

Lucille's Luscious 'Shcarole and Beans Pizza

Cousin Lucille recently shared her recipe for 'Shcarole and Beans with me. I knew immediately that her rustic, savory mixture nestled on a pizza crust under a blanket of Pecorino cheese would be out of this world! She laughed as she heard herself say, "I start it by browning some onions and garlic in a pot." Of course she laughed because we start everything that way in our family! Lucille stressed the importance of using smoked ham hocks which enhance the complexity of the flavor. If you are in the mood for some old world escarole and beans, this is the pizza for you.

6 tablespoons extra virgin olive oil, divided

1 medium yellow onion, chopped

4 cloves garlic, chopped and divided

2 smoked ham hocks

2 cups beef broth

1 bay leaf

1 cup celery-stalks and leaves, sliced

1 (15 ounce) can cannellini beans, drained and rinsed

¼ teaspoon crushed red pepper flakes

1 head escarole – approximately 1 pound

1 recipe Roasted Garlic Paste (page 170)

8 to 9 ounces prepared pizza dough at room temperature

4 ounces whole milk Mozzarella cheese, shredded

2 ounces Pecorino Romano cheese, very small chunks

freshly grated Parmigiano-Reggiano cheese

kosher salt and freshly ground black pepper to taste

1 Heat 2 tablespoons of the olive oil in a medium sauce pan over medium heat. Add onion and sauté for 2 to 3 minutes or until onions are translucent. Add half the chopped garlic and sauté, stirring for 1 to 2 minutes longer being careful not to let the garlic burn. Add ham hocks, broth, bay leaf and celery; bring to a boil. Reduce heat, cover and simmer for about 1 to 2 hours, or until hocks are tender. Remove ham hocks with a slotted spoon and place on a plate; remove pan from heat, add beans and stir to combine. Remove meat from hocks and shred with two forks or slice with a knife; add meat to bean mixture.

2 Remove and discard dark outer leaves from escarole. Cut off base, separate leaves and rinse in a large a bowl of cold water. Shake off excess moisture and pat dry with a clean kitchen towel. Stack and roll leaves; cut crosswise into 1½ inch strips, or coarsely chop. Over medium heat, warm 2 tablespoons of the olive oil in a large sauté pan. Add remaining garlic and crushed red pepper. Cook and stir for 1 minute or until garlic is fragrant and golden. Add the escarole by the handful, tossing with tongs to allow wilting of the greens before adding more. Add bean mixture to wilted escarole; remove bay leaf and stir mixture. Reduce heat to low, partially cover and gently simmer for about 20 minutes or until escarole is tender. If mixture is too soupy, uncover pan and raise heat. Boil mixture for 5 minutes to thicken. Set aside to cool for topping.

3 Roll, stretch and shape dough into an unrefined rectangular or circular shape approximately 12 by 14 inches according to basic directions. Brush both sides of dough with remaining olive oil and place on a large, rimless baking sheet or pizza peel dusted with cornmeal. Carefully lift dough and lay it on the pre-heated grill (see Grilled Pizza Primer.) Close grill lid and grill for 3 to 5 minutes or until bottom of crust is golden brown with darker grill marks. Remove from grill with tongs and place grilled side up on a flat baking sheet or pizza peel dusted with cornmeal. Spread grilled side of dough with a thin coat of roasted garlic paste and sprinkle with the Mozzarella cheese.

4 Using a large slotted spoon to drain off liquid, spoon 1 to 2 cups of the escarole, beans and ham mixture evenly over cheese. Use only enough of the mixture so there will be a bit of greens and beans on each cut piece. Overloading the dough will cause it to become soggy. Scatter chunks of Pecorino cheese over all.

5 Carefully slide pizza onto grill, turning burner directly under pizza to low. Close lid and bake for 5 minutes. Check bottom of crust by lifting the edge with tongs. If it is browning too quickly, turn off burner directly under pizza and continue baking for 5 minutes or until crust is golden and topping is bubbling.

6 Remove from heat and liberally grate Parmigiano-Reggiano cheese over all. Season with salt and freshly ground black pepper if desired.

Tip

Break off small chunks of Pecorino by inserting tip of a knife just inside the edges of the large piece of cheese and lightly twisting the knife until cheese breaks off.

Lulu's Skimpy Scampi Pizza

It is not surprising that my sister Luann is a fantastic cook since one of her fundamental beliefs is 'Everything's better with buckets of butter.' In fact, when she cooks for us she strategically places her body between us and the skillet so that we cannot witness the 'butter dump' that accompanies every dish she makes. Shrimp Scampi is one of Lu's favorite foods, but I had to use only a fraction of the butter she suggested when making this pizza. Lu would call this "skimpy on the butter," I call it scrumptious.

2 tablespoons extra virgin olive oil

4 tablespoons unsalted butter

1 shallot, minced (2 ounces)

4 cloves garlic, chopped

⅛ teaspoon crushed red pepper flakes, plus more for finishing

10 (12 to 15 count) shrimp, peeled and deveined

fresh lemon juice, one squeeze (1 to 2 teaspoons)

pinch kosher salt, or to taste

8 to 9 ounces prepared pizza dough at room temperature

8 ounces whole milk mozzarella, cut into ⅛ to ¼ inch slices

¼ cup freshly grated Parmigiano-Reggiano cheese, plus more for finishing

1 teaspoon fresh lemon zest

2 tablespoons fresh parsley leaves, chopped

1 Heat oil in a medium sauté pan over medium heat. Add butter and heat until butter foams, and then add shallots, stir and sauté for 2 to 3 minutes until translucent and just beginning to brown. Add chopped garlic and crushed red pepper flakes, stir and cook 1 minute longer until garlic is lightly browned. Do not let garlic burn as it will taste bitter.

2 Pat shrimp dry and add to sauté pan along with a squeeze of lemon juice and a pinch of salt. Cook for 1 minute (shrimp will cook further as the pizza bakes.) Remove pan from heat and remove shrimp from sauce to cool; reserve sauce for topping. Once cooled, cut shrimp crosswise into thirds and set aside for topping.

3 Roll, stretch and shape dough into a 12 to 14 inch unrefined circular shape according to basic directions. Spread dough with butter sauce in which the shrimp were cooked, using a pastry brush to distribute sauce, shallot and garlic bits evenly. Arrange sliced mozzarella over sauce and top with shrimp. Sprinkle Parmigiano-Reggiano over all.

4 Bake on a preheated Pizza Grill or on a preheated pizza stone in a 500° F. oven for 10 minutes. Bake until crust is firm and golden and top is bubbly and lightly browned.

5 Remove pizza and immediately sprinkle with crushed red pepper flakes to taste, lemon zest and chopped parsley. Grate additional Parmigiano-Reggiano cheese over all as desired. Slice and serve.

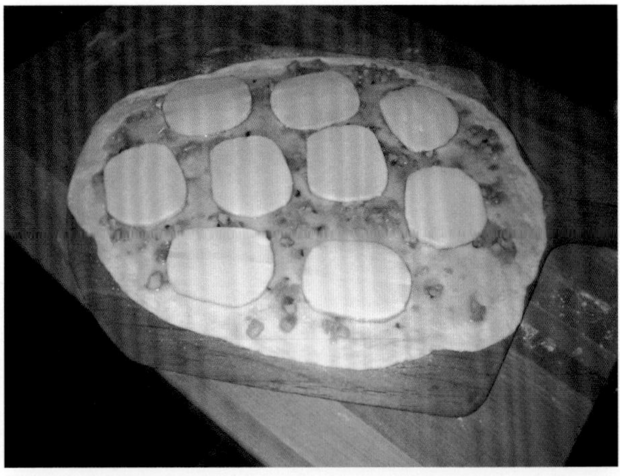

GRILLING DIRECTIONS

1. Complete steps 1 and 2 from recipe above.
2. Roll, stretch and shape dough into an unrefined 12 by 14 inch rectangular shape according to basic directions. Brush both sides of dough with 2 tablespoons of olive oil and place on a large, rimless baking sheet or pizza peel dusted with cornmeal. Carefully lift dough and lay it on the preheated grill (see Grilled Pizza Primer.) Close grill lid and grill for 3 to 5 minutes or until bottom of crust is golden brown with darker grill marks. Remove from grill with tongs and place grilled side up on a flat baking sheet or pizza peel.
3. Spread butter/shallot sauce evenly on grilled side of dough. Arrange sliced mozzarella over sauce and top with shrimp. Sprinkle with Parmigiano-Reggiano.
4. Carefully slide pizza onto grill, turning burner directly under pizza to low. Close lid and bake for 5 minutes. Check bottom of crust by lifting the edge with tongs. If it is browning too quickly, turn off burner directly under pizza and continue baking for 5 minutes or until crust is firm and golden and cheese is bubbly.
5. Complete step 5 from recipe.

Lu's Ludicrous Lobsta Bake Pizza

Knowing how much we miss the sweet taste of Maine lobsters now that we reside in Arizona, my sister Luann surprised us on a recent trip to CT by preparing an old fashioned New England Lobster bake. She kicked off the evening with an appetizer of three dozen huge shrimp swimming in cocktail sauce. Then, the ludicrous lobster bake began. She served ¼ bushel littleneck clams, ¼ bushel mussels, 15 one and one half pound lobsters, 4 dozen ears of corn and enough melted butter to float a small fishing boat. You may be asking yourself why I call this 'ludicrous'. Well, truth be told, there were not 12 guests, not even 10. No, there were only 5 of us at her table that night! Needless to say, we all ate until we could eat no more! This pizza is my version of Lu's lobster bake. It takes a bit of extra preparation time, but you will experience the taste of a traditional New England lobster bake and that should make it worth your while.

8 ounces small red bliss potatoes

12 littleneck clams in their shells; or 1 can (6.5 ounces) whole clams, drained; like Trader Joe's® Maine Whole Cherrystone Clams

6 tablespoons unsalted butter

2 cloves garlic, smashed

1 tablespoon chopped fresh flat leaf parsley

1 tablespoon chopped fresh chives

kosher salt

freshly ground black pepper

9 to 10 ounces prepared pizza dough at room temperature

4 ounces whole milk mozzarella cheese, shredded

4 ounces fontina cheese, shredded

2 tablespoons freshly grated Parmigiano-Reggiano cheese, plus additional for finishing

1 ear corn, roasted; or 1/3 cup frozen roasted corn, thawed. Recommended brand – Trader Joe's®

8 halves Slow Roasted Tomatoes (page 171) cut in half lengthwise

4 ounces linguica cooked and cut crosswise into ¼ inch slices; substitute Spanish chorizo or kielbasa

8 ounces cooked lobster meat, cut into bite size chunks

sea salt

lemon zest and juice, parsley and chives for garnish

1 Place whole, unpeeled potatoes in a saucepan and cover with water. Add 1 teaspoon kosher salt and bring water to a boil. Reduce heat and simmer 15 to 20 minutes or until potatoes are tender, not mushy when pierced with the tip of a knife. Drain and set aside. While clams are cooking in step 2, cut potatoes into small dice.

2 Rinse clams and place into a large pot of cold water. Scrub each clam with a vegetable brush. Rinse and refrigerate until ready to use. About 15 minutes before assembling pizza, place clams in a large pot. Add one to two cups water. Cover pot and bring to a boil. Lower heat and simmer clams for 5 to 7 minutes or until shells open. Discard any clams that do not open. Remove clams from pot with a slotted spoon and remove cooked clams from shells. Set aside for topping.

3 In a small skillet, melt butter over medium heat. Add smashed garlic and reduce heat to low. Allow garlic to cook for 4 to 6 minutes in the barely simmering butter. Watch carefully to prevent garlic from burning. Add parsley and chives; stir a few times. Remove from heat and season with salt and pepper to taste. Set skillet aside.

4 Roll, stretch and shape dough into an unrefined rectangular shape approximately 12 by 14 inches, according to basic directions. Place on a pizza peel that has been dusted with cornmeal. Brush dough with 2 to 3 tablespoons of the melted herb butter.

5 Combine mozzarella, fontina and Parmigiano-Reggiano cheese in a medium bowl. Scatter half of the cheese mixture over the buttered dough. Top with clams and roasted corn.

6 Arrange roasted tomato pieces, diced potatoes and sausage slices over pizza. Top with remaining cheese mixture.

7 Bake on a preheated Pizza Grill or preheated pizza stone in a 500° F. oven for 10 to 12 minutes, rotating crust after 4 minutes to prevent sticking. Bake until crust is firm and cheese is bubbly.

8 While pizza is baking, heat the skillet containing the remaining herb butter over medium-low heat. Add lobster pieces and heat for 2 to 3 minutes or until lobster is just warmed through. Cover pan and remove from heat.

9 Remove pizza from heat. Top with warmed lobster pieces and remaining butter (if desired.) Grate Parmigiano-Reggiano cheese over all and season to taste with sea salt and freshly ground black pepper. Zest lemon over pizza and drizzle with a bit of the fresh lemon juice. Garnish with chopped parsley and chives. Cut and serve immediately.

Although you won't have to spread newspaper before eating your pizza - you may need to use a fork and knife. Lobsta bakes can be quite messy!

Mark's Yellow Fingers Pizza

From the time my nephew Mark was a young boy; his favorite food was "Chicken That Makes Your Fingers Turn Yellow." He named the dish for obvious reasons; it DID make his fingers turn yellow. His mom, my sister Elaine regularly cooked up huge amounts of this chicken for Mark; yet he never tired of it. Even though Mark is in his 40s, he still asks his mother if she will make him a batch of 'chicken that makes your fingers turn yellow' every time she visits him and his family in Oregon. It never ceases to amaze me how quickly we can become the 'kids sitting at Mommy's kitchen table' when we smell, taste or even just reminisce about our favorite childhood foods.

- **1 recipe Classic Caramelized Onions (page 169)**
- **1 recipe Yogurt-Cucumber Sauce (recipe follows)**
- **1 cup plain low fat yogurt**
- **2 cloves garlic, minced**
- **½ teaspoon kosher salt**
- **¼ teaspoon freshly ground black pepper**
- **½ teaspoon turmeric**
- **½ teaspoon ground ginger**
- **1 teaspoon Garam Masala**
- **1 tablespoon freshly squeezed lemon juice**
- **2 chicken thighs, boneless and skinless (8 ounces total weight)**
- **3 tablespoons extra virgin olive oil, divided**
- **2 tablespoons unsalted butter**
- **4 large white mushrooms, thickly sliced**
- **9 ounces prepared whole wheat or regular pizza dough at room temperature**
- **3 to 4 ounces whole milk mozzarella cheese, shredded**
- **3 to 4 ounces extra sharp white cheddar cheese, shredded**

1. In a medium bowl, combine yogurt, garlic, salt, black pepper, turmeric, ginger, and Garam Masala; stir in lemon juice. Cut each chicken thigh into 3 or 4 wide strips; add to yogurt mixture and toss until chicken is thoroughly coated. Cover bowl and marinate in refrigerator for at least 2 hours.
2. Heat 2 tablespoons of the olive oil in a medium sauté pan over medium-high heat. Remove chicken from marinade, allowing extra marinade to drip off. Sauté chicken on medium high for 5 to 6 minutes per side, or until chicken is lightly browned and juices run clear. Remove chicken, cut into small pieces and set aside for topping. Chicken can also be grilled over medium high heat for 5 to 6 minutes per side.
3. Melt butter in a medium skillet over medium-high heat. Add mushrooms and sauté for 5 minutes, or until just beginning to brown. Set aside.
4. Roll, stretch and shape dough into an unrefined 12 by 14 inch rectangular or circular shape, according to basic directions. Brush edges of dough with remaining tablespoon of olive oil.
5. Spread an even layer of caramelized onions over dough, leaving a one half inch border. Combine mozzarella and cheddar cheese in a small bowl and sprinkle half the mixture over the onions.
6. Top cheese with an even layer of chicken pieces; then mushrooms and remaining cheese.
7. Bake on a preheated Pizza Grill or on a preheated pizza stone in a 500° F. oven for 10 to 12 minutes, rotating pizza after 4 minutes to prevent sticking. Bake until crust is firm and golden and cheese is bubbly.
8. Remove from heat, spoon small dollops of yogurt sauce over top of pizza. Cut and serve.

Yogurt-Cucumber Sauce

½ cup plain yogurt, low fat or regular

¼ cup finely minced, peeled and seeded cucumber

2 tablespoons finely minced sweet onion

⅛ teaspoon curry powder

kosher salt and freshly ground black pepper, to taste

1 Combine all ingredients in a small bowl.

2 Cover and refrigerate until needed for finishing pizza.

Matt's 'Mmm Haaam' Pizza

Delicious hunks of ham...hot, cold, in a casserole, on a sandwich, or any which way is a dream come true for Matthew. Now Matt can enjoy his favorite Easter dinner of baked ham and cheesy garlic potatoes any time. Bake up this Mmm Haaam Pizza and you too can enjoy that special dinner any night of the week.

2 medium Yukon gold potatoes, washed (approximately 8 ounces)

kosher salt

freshly ground black pepper

8 to 9 ounces prepared pizza dough at room temperature

2 tablespoons extra virgin olive oil

1 recipe Roasted Garlic Paste (page 170)

8 ounces extra sharp cheddar cheese, shredded and divided

4 ounces country baked ham, cut into slivers

¼ cup frozen peas, thawed

¼ cup heavy cream

1 Place potatoes into a saucepan and add water to cover. Bring to a boil over high heat. Lower heat to medium and simmer until potatoes are just tender, about 20 minutes. Drain and set aside. When cool enough to handle, cut into ⅛ inch thick slices; season lightly with salt and pepper and reserve for topping.

2 Roll, stretch and shape dough into an unrefined rectangular or circular shape approximately 12 to 14 inches according to the basic directions. Brush dough with olive oil and spread with a thin layer of garlic paste. Sprinkle with 6 ounces of the cheddar cheese.

3 Arrange potato slices in an attractive pattern over cheese and scatter ham slivers and peas among the potato slices. Sprinkle with remaining 2 ounces of cheese and drizzle with heavy cream.

4 Bake on a preheated Pizza Grill or on a preheated pizza stone in a 500° F. oven, rotating after 4 minutes to prevent sticking. Bake for 10 to 12 minutes or until crust is firm and golden and cheese is bubbly across entire top of pizza.

5 Remove from heat, cut into squares or wedges as desired. Serve immediately.

Tip

You can also use deli ham off the bone cut into narrow strips.

Matt's Mollusk Madness Pizza

Matt mainly munches mollusks as appetizers; scallops wrapped in bacon are a favorite, unless he is in New York City at lunch time. It is then that Matt seriously scoffs down a bucket or two of mussels, another of his mollusk friends. Matt prefers mussels to oysters, but Mom maintains that breaded, lightly sautéed oysters, not mussels, would be an outrageous addition to Matt's Mollusk Madness Pizza.

8 to 9 ounces prepared pizza dough at room temperature

1 tablespoon fresh thyme leaves, chopped

½ cup freshly grated Parmigiano-Reggiano cheese divided

2 tablespoons extra virgin olive oil

2 tablespoons Roasted Garlic Paste (page 170)

6 large sea scallops, rinsed and patted dry

6 slices bacon, cut into ½ inch dice

¾ cup Basic Sauce All' Amatriciana (page 165)

6 ounces whole milk mozzarella cheese, shredded (approximately 1½ cups)

2 tablespoons fresh flat leaf parsley, chopped

crushed red pepper flakes

1. Knead thyme and ¼ cup grated Parmigiano-Reggiano cheese into prepared dough and set aside until ready to assemble pizza.
2. In a small bowl, stir olive oil into garlic paste and set aside.
3. Heat a medium sauté pan over medium-high heat. When pan is hot, add bacon and cook. Stirring to separate the pieces. Cook until all the fat has been rendered and bacon is very lightly browned, about 7 minutes. Remove with a slotted spoon. Drain on a paper towel lined plate and reserve for topping.
4. Slice each scallop into 2 or 3 disks, about ⅜ of an inch thick. Sauté in hot bacon fat for one minute, stirring to coat pieces. Remove from fat and drain on a paper towel lined plate. When cool enough to handle, cut each disc in half, if desired. Reserve for topping.
5. Roll, stretch and shape dough into an unrefined 12 to 14 inch circular shape according to basic directions. Brush dough with roasted garlic and olive oil mixture. Spread All' Amatriciana sauce on dough, using only enough to lightly cover dough. Sprinkle 1 cup mozzarella cheese over sauce and top with bacon pieces.
6. Arrange scallops evenly over pizza. Combine remaining ½ cup mozzarella with the remaining ¼ cup Parmigiano-Reggiano and sprinkle over entire pizza.
7. Bake on a preheated Pizza Grill or on a preheated pizza stone in a 500° F. oven, turning after 4 minutes to prevent sticking. Bake for 10 to 12 minutes or until crust is firm, cheese is bubbly and scallops are cooked through. Remove from heat and sprinkle with chopped parsley and, if you desire more heat, crushed red pepper flakes. Cut and serve immediately.

Tip

Stack bacon slices, cut lengthwise in half and crosswise into ½ inch pieces.

Mitchie's Mounds of Chili Pizza

My sister Karen Michelle, aka Mitchie, loved my mother's chili. Karen laughs as she recalls her memory of my mother standing at the stove stirring a huge pot of chili saying, 'I wish I had four boys (instead of four girls) because the boys could eat a lot more than you girls.' Well, Mitchie would eat several bowls of this fabulous chili...probably mostly out of guilt! She claims she did love it though. My mother never got her wish of having four boys, but she did have four girls who could give any guy a run for his money when it came to eating great food!

1½ cups Beef and Beans Chili at room temperature (recipe follows)

8 to 9 ounces prepared pizza dough at room temperature

2 tablespoons extra virgin olive oil

4 ounces shredded 4 cheese Mexican blend, divided (approximately 1 cup)

1 ear roasted corn or ½ cup frozen roasted corn, thawed (recommended brand – Trader Joe's®)

2 ounces asadero, Manchego or jack cheese, shredded (approximately ½ cup)

sour cream

¼ cup scallions, white and light green parts thinly sliced

1 Prepare Beef and Beans Chili and set aside to cool.

2 Roll, stretch and shape dough into an unrefined circular or rectangular shape approximately 12 by 14 inches, according to basic directions. Brush dough with olive oil and sprinkle with 3 ounces (¾ cup) of the Mexican cheese mix. Spoon the room temperature chili over the cheese; sprinkle roasted corn kernels over chili and top with remaining Mexican and asadero cheese.

3 Bake on a preheated Pizza Grill or on a preheated pizza stone in a 500° F. oven, rotating after 4 minutes to prevent sticking. Bake for 10 to 12 minutes or until crust is firm and golden and topping is bubbly.

4 Remove from grill or oven and place small dollops of sour cream randomly over top of pizza. Sprinkle with scallions; cut and serve immediately.

Beef and Beans Chili - Yield approximately 6 cups

2 tablespoons extra virgin olive oil

1½ pounds ground beef – 80% lean

2 yellow onions, chopped (approximately 2 cups)

2 cloves garlic, chopped

1 (28 ounce) can crushed tomatoes

1 tablespoon chili powder

½ teaspoon ancho or chipotle chili powder – use up to 1 teaspoon for extra smoky heat [I use ½ teaspoon of each]

1 teaspoon cumin

½ teaspoon Mexican oregano

1 teaspoon kosher salt

½ teaspoon freshly ground black pepper

1 (16 ounce) can red kidney beans, drained and rinsed

1 Heat olive oil in a large sauté pan over medium high heat. Add beef and cook, breaking beef apart as it browns. Cook until beef loses its pink color, approximately 4 minutes; add onions and cook, stirring often, until beef and onions are lightly browned, about 4 minutes. Add garlic and sauté 1 minute longer.

2 Add tomatoes, chili powders, cumin, oregano, salt, pepper. Stir to combine then stir in beans; bring to a boil.

3 Lower heat to medium low; simmer covered for 30 minutes, stirring occasionally. Partially uncover and simmer 30 minutes longer over medium low heat until thickened. Cool before using on pizza.

COOK'S NOTE: *Chili can be prepared up to a few days in advance. Cool, cover and refrigerate until one half hour before you are ready to use; then bring to room temperature.*

Peperonata and Sausage Pizza

~

Pizza Salsiccia Peperonata

The aroma from this pizza sitting in the center of our kitchen table brings to mind my five amazing Italian aunts and the hours spent in their kitchens while pots of Sunday 'gravy', 'scharole and beans or pasta 'fazool' slowly simmered on the back stove burners. Heavenly aromas filled their homes and our hearts. Take time to make this tasty pizza...your family and friends will love you for it.

8 ounces bulk sweet Italian sausage (bulk chicken sausage can be substituted for a lighter version)

8 to 9 ounces prepared pizza dough at room temperature

2 tablespoons extra virgin olive oil

½ cup Basil Pesto (page 173) or use a good quality purchased basil pesto

6 ounces whole milk mozzarella, shredded and divided

1 cup Peperonata, recipe follows

3 tablespoons freshly grated Parmigiano-Reggiano cheese, plus extra for finishing

1. Heat a 12 inch sauté pan over medium high heat. Add sausage and cook for 5 minutes, breaking apart and stirring as it cooks. Drain oil from sausage and cool slightly. Sausage should be cooked, but not browned.
2. Roll, stretch and shape dough into an unrefined 12 to 14 inch rectangular or circular shape according to basic directions and brush with olive oil.
3. Spread a thin layer of basil pesto over dough and cover with ½ cup of the mozzarella cheese.
4. Distribute peperonata evenly over entire crust so that all slices will contain a bit of each of the ingredients.
5. Scatter cooked sausage over pizza and top with remaining mozzarella cheese and grated Parmigiano-Reggiano.
6. Bake for 10 minutes on a preheated Pizza Grill or on a preheated pizza stone in a 500° F. oven, rotating after 4 minutes to prevent sticking. Bake until crust is firm and golden brown and top is bubbly. Remove from heat and immediately grate additional Parmigiano over top before cutting.

Peperonata - Yield approximately 4 cups

- **3 tablespoons extra virgin olive oil**
- **8 ounces yellow onion, sliced ¼ inch thick**
- **½ teaspoon sea salt, or to taste**
- **1 pound bell peppers, a combination of red, yellow and green**
- **2 fresh peeled tomatoes, cored seeded and diced**
- **¼ cup kalamata olives, pitted**
- **2 tablespoons capers, drained**
- **1 tablespoon balsamic vinegar**
- **1 clove garlic**
- **1 tablespoon fresh parsley leaves**

1. Heat oil in a large sauté pan over medium high heat. Add onions and salt; lower heat to medium low and cook slowly for 20 to 30 minutes, or until onions are soft and translucent.
2. While onion cooks, core and clean peppers. Quarter peppers lengthwise then cut in half crosswise or cut peppers into eights lengthwise, if preferred. Add peppers to onions, stir to combine. Cover pan and cook on medium to medium-low heat for about 20 minutes until softened.
3. Add tomatoes, stir to combine and cook for another 10 minutes or until most of the moisture evaporates and mixture thickens.
4. Stir in olives and capers. Drizzle with balsamic vinegar and allow it to evaporate; raise the heat a bit if necessary to facilitate evaporation.
5. Chop garlic and parsley together, add to the pan and stir to combine. Remove from heat and set aside to cool.

NOTE: *Peperonata is best if made ahead. Keeps in the refrigerator in a tightly sealed container up to 4 days.*

Tip

To peel tomatoes, carefully plunge them into boiling water for 15 to 30 seconds. Remove with a slotted spoon and cool until you can handle them. Peel from stem to bottom with a paring knife.

Perla's Puttanesca Pizza

Auntie Perla was famous in our family for her pasta puttanesca. She loved anything salty and spicy especially if it was on pasta; so it comes as no surprise that puttanesca style pasta was one of her favorites. I remember how difficult it was to consume a serving of that pasta...it tasted like a salt lick. Of course, with the exception of my mother, who rarely added salt to her recipes, the 'grown-ups' loved Perla's puttanesca pasta. For this pizza, I sauté and mash the anchovies in oil which gives them a wonderful nutty, less salty taste. To further cut down on the saltiness, you can eliminate the whole anchovies when topping your Puttanesca Pizza.

¼ cup extra virgin olive oil

6 anchovy fillets packed in oil, plus several for topping

8 to 9 ounces prepared pizza dough at room temperature

¾ cup Basic Sauce All' Amatriciana (page 165)

4 to 6 ounces asiago cheese, shredded (approximately 1 to 1½ cups)

½ cup Italian black olives, pitted and roughly chopped (6 to 8 Gaeta olives)

¼ cup capers, drained and patted dry

½ teaspoon dried oregano

¼ cup Pecorino Romano cheese, freshly grated; plus more for finishing

2 tablespoons fresh flat leaf parsley, chopped

crushed red pepper flakes

1 Heat olive oil in a 10 inch skillet over medium-high heat. Add anchovies and sauté, mashing fillets and stirring until they 'melt' into the oil, about 2 to 3 minutes. Set aside to cool.

2 Roll, stretch and shape dough into an unrefined 12 to 14 inch circular shape according to basic directions. Brush dough with cooled oil/anchovy mixture, then spread the All' Amatricana sauce over dough, using only enough to lightly coat dough.

3 Sprinkle the asiago cheese over the sauce and scatter olives and capers over all. Sprinkle with oregano and Pecorino Romano cheese. Arrange remaining anchovy fillets over the top of the pizza. These can be omitted if you prefer a more subtle anchovy flavor.

4 Bake on a preheated Pizza Grill or on a preheated pizza stone in a 500° F. oven for 10 minutes, rotating pizza after 4 minutes to prevent sticking. Bake until crust is firm and golden and cheese is bubbly. To bake this pizza directly on gas grill grates, follow directions on next page.

5 Remove from heat and immediately grate additional Pecorino Romano cheese over pizza. Sprinkle with chopped parsley and crushed red pepper flakes to taste. Cut and serve.

GRILLING DIRECTIONS

1. Stretch dough into a 12 by 14 inch rectangular shape making it quite thin.
2. Brush both sides of dough with olive oil and place on a large, rimless baking sheet or pizza peel that has been lightly dusted with cornmeal.
3. Carefully lift dough and lay it on the preheated grill (see Grilled Pizza Primer.) Close grill lid and grill for 3 to 5 minutes or until bottom of crust is lightly golden brown with darker grill marks. Remove from grill with tongs and place grilled side up on a flat baking sheet or pizza peel.
4. Proceed with step 2 above from brushing dough with oil/anchovy mixture through step 3.
5. Carefully slide pizza onto grill, turning burner directly under pizza to low. Close lid and bake for 5 minutes. Check bottom of crust by lifting the edge with tongs. If it is browning too quickly, turn off burner under pizza and continue baking for 4 to 5 minutes. Carefully remove to pizza peel or flat cookie sheet. Proceed with step 5 above.

Porky Pine Pizza

Growing up in Connecticut, fall was my favorite season. I loved everything about it from the vibrant foliage, to the crispness in the air, to the amazing aromas that would envelop me each day as I returned from school and walked into my mother's kitchen. Dutch apple cake was one of her favorites to bake in the fall and I would actually beg her for the tiniest sliver when it came out of the oven. She also baked the most incredible pork chops that were bursting with her special bread stuffing containing bits of onion, corn kernels and dried apricots. The aroma of pork with its fruity stuffing roasting in the oven still titillates all my senses. Pop a piece of 'Porky Pine Pizza' into your mouth and savor the flavor any time of the year.

8 to 9 ounces prepared pizza dough at room temperature

1 tablespoon slivered dried apricots (optional)

1 tablespoon fresh sage leaves, chopped; plus additional whole leaves for garnish

2 links sweet Italian sausage – use up to 8 ounces

½ to 1 cup Apricot Chutney (recipe follows) or use good quality purchased chutney

1 cup fontina cheese, shredded and divided (approximately 4 ounces)

¼ cup frozen corn kernels, thawed

3 tablespoons pine nuts

1. Knead slivered apricots and chopped sage into dough. Set aside.
2. Heat a 10 inch skillet over medium high heat. Remove sausage from casing and cook for 5 minutes, breaking it apart and stirring as it cooks. Sausage should be cooked, but not browned.
3. Roll, stretch and shape dough into an unrefined 12 to 14 inch circular shape according to basic directions. Spread dough with enough room temperature apricot chutney to cover and sprinkle with ½ cup fontina cheese.
4. Distribute sausage and corn kernels over the pizza and sprinkle the remaining ½ cup fontina over all. Scatter pine nuts over the cheese.
5. Bake on a preheated Pizza Grill or on a preheated pizza stone in a 500° F. oven for 10 minutes, rotating pizza after 4 minutes to prevent sticking. Bake until crust is firm and golden and top is bubbly.

Tip

To toast mustard seeds, heat a small skillet over medium heat. Place seeds in the skillet and heat, shaking pan often until the seeds begin to pop and are lightly golden brown. Watch carefully, as they can quickly burn.

Apricot Chutney - Yield 3 cups

- **2 cups dried apricots**
- **2 tablespoons extra virgin olive oil**
- **1 large yellow onion, finely chopped**
- **2 cloves garlic, minced**
- **2 tablespoons mustard seeds, lightly toasted**
- **1 tablespoon peeled and minced or grated fresh ginger**
- **⅛ teaspoon crushed red pepper flakes**
- **½ cup apple cider vinegar**
- **⅓ cup granulated sugar**
- **kosher salt to taste**

1. Place apricots in a 1.5 quart saucepan and cover with water by ½ inch (approximately 2 cups.) Bring to a boil, cover and immediately turn off heat. Allow to stand covered for 30 minutes, or until apricots are somewhat softened. Drain and chop coarsely.
2. In a 2 quart saucepan, heat oil over medium high heat and cook onion until soft and lightly browned, 7 to 9 minutes. Add garlic, mustard seeds, ginger and crushed red pepper and cook for 2 minutes.
3. Add apricots, vinegar and sugar, stir to combine. Bring to a boil then reduce heat to medium-low, cover and simmer, stirring occasionally for 30 minutes or until apricots are soft and mixture is slightly thickened. (Add water as needed to prevent mixture from drying out before apricots are soft.)
4. Remove from heat and season to taste with salt. Bring to room temperature.
5. Refrigerate, covered for up to 5 days.

Serve at room temperature.

Save the Day Olé Pizza

*My favorite food for unexpected company is **anything** that I can put together on a moments notice. This pizza really did 'save the day' for me. I had been testing recipes for several days, when friends unexpectedly dropped by for a visit. Just like my Italian aunties of the old days, the first thought that popped into my head was, 'what can I offer them to eat?' Old habits die hard! My mind raced, left over Sofrito-yes, Serrano ham-no, garlic-always! I had some shrimp marinating in the refrigerator for dinner, but how to stretch eight ounces of shrimp to feed four adults was a quandary. Then it hit me – D'OUGH – make a pizza!*

8 ounces shrimp (16 to 20 count), peeled and deveined

2 cloves garlic, minced

4 tablespoons Spanish olive oil, divided; plus more for drizzling

8 to 9 ounces prepared pizza dough at room temperature

½ cup Sofrito - Basic Spanish Tomato Sauce (page 166)

6 ounces Manchego cheese, shredded and divided

½ cup small Spanish manzanilla olives; drained, patted dry and sliced or chopped

4 scallions, white and light green parts sliced thinly on an angle

Cotija cheese – to taste

kosher salt and freshly ground black pepper to taste

1 Pat shrimp dry and place in a plastic zip top bag with garlic and 2 tablespoons of the olive oil. Seal bag securely and massage oil and garlic into shrimp. Refrigerate for at least 30 minutes or up to 4 hours.

2 Grill shrimp in an even layer directly on grill grates or on a perforated grill pan over high heat for 1 to 2 minutes per side, or until shrimp just begin to turn pink. This can be done up to 30 minutes before assembling pizza. When cool enough to handle, cut crosswise into thirds.

3 Roll, stretch and shape dough into an unrefined rectangular shape approximately 12 by 14 inches according to basic directions. Brush both sides of dough with remaining 2 tablespoons olive oil and place on a large, rimless baking sheet or pizza peel that has been lightly dusted with cornmeal. Carefully lift dough and lay it on the preheated grill (see Grilled Pizza Primer.) Close grill lid and grill for 3 to 5 minutes or until bottom of crust is golden brown with darker grill marks. Remove from grill with tongs and place grilled side up on a flat baking sheet or pizza peel.

4 Spread grilled side of dough with a generous half cup of Sofrito to within ½ inch of edge of dough. Top with one half the Manchego cheese. Scatter olives, shrimp and scallions over all. Top with remaining Manchego cheese.

5 Carefully slide pizza onto grill, turning burner directly under pizza to low. Close lid and bake for 5 minutes. Check bottom of crust by lifting the edge with tongs. If it is browning too quickly, turn off burner directly under pizza and continue baking for 5 minutes or until crust is firm and golden and cheese is melted.

6 Remove from heat and immediately drizzle with Spanish olive oil and grate Cotija cheese over top of pizza as desired. Season with kosher salt and ground pepper. Cut and serve immediately.

COOK'S NOTE: *Fortunately, the day of my unexpected company, I had a few balls of dough in the refrigerator. I always keep several packages of pizza dough in the freezer for emergencies. I have defrosted and used dough that was frozen for four months and it was as fresh as the day I made it!*

TO BAKE ON A PIZZA GRILL OR IN AN OVEN: Roll, stretch and shape dough into an irregular 12 by 14 inch rectangular shape according to basic directions. Brush only one side with olive oil. Spread with Sofrito and scatter half the cheese evenly over the sauce. Top with olives, shrimp and scallions. Sprinkle remaining cheese over all.

Bake on a preheated Pizza Grill or on a preheated pizza stone in a 500° F. oven, rotating pizza after the first four minutes to prevent sticking. Bake for 10 to 12 minutes or until crust is firm and golden and cheese is melted.

Follow step 6.

NON-OLIVE VARIATION: Use two tablespoons capers, drained and patted dry and ¼ cup thinly sliced onions in place of olives and scallions. This suggestion comes from my brother-in –law Ervin, who carefully removed each olive from his pizza slices because, unbeknownst to me, he detests olives.

Shrimp and Red Pepper Pesto Pizza

Over the years, I have served shrimp cocktail more times than I can count. Eventually, boredom set in and boiled shrimp with no frills cocktail sauce held no charm. I began experimenting with new sauces and dips, trying everything from sickeningly sweet to killer spicy – learning the hard way to use wasabi powder in moderation. Realizing that the shrimp also played a part in this lackluster appetizer, I marinated them in garlic, oil, salt and crushed red pepper, grilled them and dipped them into a fragrant, nutty roasted red pepper pesto. Success! The combination was incredible and thus became my go to shrimp cocktail appetizer. When you bite into a piece of this pizza, remember that this extraordinary taste began as an unremarkable shrimp cocktail.

8 (16 to 20 count) ounces shrimp

2 tablespoons extra virgin olive oil, plus more for brushing dough

2 cloves garlic, minced

¼ teaspoon crushed red pepper flakes, plus more for finishing

8 to 9 ounces prepared pizza dough at room temperature

½ cup Roasted Red Pepper Pesto (page 174)

4 ounces whole milk mozzarella cheese, shredded

½ small red bell pepper, cored, seeded and cut into thin strips

½ small onion, cut into thin strips

1 ounce freshly grated Parmigiano-Reggiano cheese

4 to 5 fresh basil leaves, torn into small pieces

kosher salt

freshly grated lemon zest

1 In a small bowl or quart size zip-top plastic bag, combine 2 tablespoons of the olive oil, garlic and crushed red pepper. Peel, devein and rinse shrimp; pat dry. Slice each shrimp in half from head to tail and stir into garlic/oil marinade. Refrigerate for at least 30 minutes.

2 Roll stretch and shape dough into an unrefined 12 to 14 inch rectangular or circular shape according to basic directions. Place on a pizza peel or rimless baking sheet that has been dusted with cornmeal. Brush outer edge of dough with olive oil; spread an even layer of red pepper pesto over dough to within one half inch from edge and sprinkle with mozzarella and/or Manchego cheese.

3 Remove shrimp from marinade, allowing any excess to drip off. Arrange over the cheese in a single layer; place pepper strips and onion between the shrimp. Sprinkle Parmigiano-Reggiano over all.

4 Bake on a preheated Pizza Grill or on a preheated pizza stone in a 500° F. oven for 10 to 12 minutes, rotating pizza after 4 minutes to prevent sticking. Bake until crust is firm and golden and cheese is bubbly.

5 Remove from heat and top with torn basil leaves. Season with crushed red pepper flakes and kosher salt to taste. Grate fresh lemon zest over all as desired. Cut and serve immediately.

Tip

You can use Manchego cheese in place of the mozzarella, or use a combination of both. Manchego cheese has a buttery texture and will add a slight piquancy to your pizza.

GRILLING DIRECTIONS:

Preheat gas grill (see Grilled Pizza Primer.) Complete step 1. Shape dough as per step 2. Brush both sides of dough with olive oil and place on a large, rimless baking sheet or pizza peel dusted with cornmeal. Carefully lift dough and lay it on the preheated grill, turning burner directly under dough to low. Close grill lid and grill for 3 to 5 minutes or until bottom of crust is golden brown with darker grill marks. Remove from grill with tongs and place grilled side up on a flat baking sheet or pizza peel. Brush grilled side of dough with remaining oil, spread pesto over dough then complete step 3. Carefully slide pizza onto grill, keeping burner directly under pizza to low. Close lid and bake for 5 minutes. Check bottom of crust by lifting the edge with tongs. If it is browning too quickly, turn off burner directly under pizza and continue baking for 5 minutes or until shrimp are cooked, crust is golden and cheese is melted. Complete step 5.

Sonny Boy's Sensational Salami Pizza

My Sonny Boy…I made him an offer he couldn't refuse. I promised to make him a pizza that replicated his favorite deli 'sangweech'. This one comes very close. Mangia!

8 to 9 ounces prepared pizza dough at room temperature

2 tablespoons oil (1 tablespoon olive oil and 1 tablespoon roasted red pepper oil combined)

4 ounces whole milk mozzarella cheese, shredded

6 1 inch strips Caramelized Sweet Peppers (recipe follows)

4 ounces Genoa salami, thinly sliced and cut into quarters

2 ounces sharp provolone cheese, thinly sliced and cut into 1 inch strips

1 tablespoon capers, drained and patted dry

roasted red pepper oil for drizzling

3 to 4 fresh basil leaves, torn

dried oregano to taste

crushed red pepper flakes

1. Brush dough with oil mixture; scatter mozzarella cheese to within ½ inch from edge of dough.
2. Arrange salami and pepper pieces over cheese and sprinkle with capers.
3. Top with provolone cheese strips.
4. Drizzle with a small amount of roasted red pepper oil.
5. Bake on a preheated Pizza Grill or on a preheated pizza stone in a 500° F. oven for 10 to 12 minutes, or until cheese is bubbly and crust is lightly browned. Rotate pizza after four minutes to prevent sticking.
6. Immediately after removing from oven, brush outer crust with oil. Sprinkle pizza with freshly torn basil leaves, dried oregano and crushed red pepper flakes, if desired.

COOK'S NOTE: *Double the amount of roasted peppers when assembling this pizza, keeping all other ingredients the same. The result is an amazingly different pizza – a burst of sweetness from the caramelized peppers with a slightly salty undertone from the salami.*

Caramelized Bell Peppers – Yield approximately 24 strips

1 large yellow bell pepper

2 large red bell peppers

3 tablespoons extra virgin olive oil

1 teaspoon sugar

1 tablespoon good balsamic vinegar

coarse salt to taste

1. Core and seed peppers. Cut the peppers into 1 inch wide strips.
2. Heat oil in a large sauté pan and add peppers. Cover and sauté over medium heat for 20 minutes. Stir occasionally.
3. Sprinkle peppers with sugar and add balsamic vinegar; stir to combine.
4. Sauté covered for 5 to 7 minutes longer or until peppers are somewhat tender and lightly browned. Peppers will continue to cook on the pizza.
5. Finish with coarse salt to taste.

Spana~KO~Pizza

Spanakopita is a surprisingly savory strudel of sorts that is to Greeks what pizza is to Americans. My first and only attempt at making it for my husband, whose mother was Greek, was somewhat of a failure. My problem was that I did not know how to work with phyllo dough. The fine sheets tore as I handled them, came apart as I brushed butter on them and dried out completely while waiting to be used. The spinach filling was quite good though, and I baked it in a casserole, admitting defeat. Many years have passed since then and my fear of phyllo stands firm. This pizza is my way of 'thumbing my nose' so to speak at phyllo. That savory spinach filling on a pizza crust satisfies sufficiently – who needs phyllo?

1 (10 ounce) package frozen chopped spinach, thawed

¼ cup extra virgin olive oil, divided

½ cup finely chopped onion

4 scallions, white and green parts, chopped

2 tablespoons finely chopped fresh flat leaf parsley

2 tablespoons fresh dill, finely chopped

½ teaspoon freshly grated nutmeg

½ teaspoon kosher salt

½ teaspoon freshly ground black pepper

4 ounces feta cheese, crumbled

8 to 9 ounces prepared pizza dough at room temperature (regular or whole wheat)

4 ounces whole milk mozzarella cheese, shredded

¼ cup pine nuts

1 to 2 ounces freshly grated Parmigiano-Reggiano cheese

lemon zest freshly grated on a Microplane® – to taste

1. Drain spinach by placing in a colander in a sink and pressing spinach with the back of a large spoon or by wringing spinach in a clean kitchen towel over a bowl or sink.
2. Heat 2 tablespoons of the oil in a medium sauté pan; add onion and cook over medium heat for about 5 minutes, or until translucent. Add scallions and sauté for 2 minutes; stir spinach, parsley, dill, nutmeg, salt and pepper into the onion mixture. Cook, stirring often until any excess liquid cooks off. Cool slightly, then lightly fold in the feta cheese and set aside for topping.
3. Roll, stretch and shape dough into an unrefined 12 by 14 inch rectangular or circular shape according to basic directions. Brush dough with remaining 2 tablespoons of olive oil.
4. Scatter mozzarella cheese over dough in an even layer and distribute spinach/feta mixture over cheese. Sprinkle pine nuts over spinach and top with grated Parmigiano-Regianno cheese.
5. Bake on a preheated Pizza Grill or on a preheated pizza stone in a 500° F. oven, rotating after 4 minutes to prevent sticking. Bake for 10 to 12 minutes or until crust is firm and golden and cheese is bubbling under the spinach mixture.
6. Remove from heat and garnish with lemon zest to taste. Cut and serve immediately.

Sumptuous Summer Tomato Pizza

It happened suddenly one summer day. I was walking through a wonderful farmer's market with my daughter while visiting her in New Haven, CT when I spotted the most spectacularly plump, ripe red tomatoes. As I eyed those red beauties, a gentle summer breeze wafted through the market, softly caressing my face and carrying on its wings the heavenly smell of pizza baking at nearby Pepe's Pizzeria. My mind raced. Farmer's market...plump tomatoes, specialty cheeses, fresh bunches of aromatic basil...PIZZA! I could hardly wait to get back to Jen's place to assemble this summer beauty. Since I had not brought my outdoor Pizza Grill with me from Arizona, I had to improvise. That cheese and tomato beauty went directly onto the grates of her gas grill and that evening we reveled in the simple pleasures of summer.

8 to 9 ounces prepared pizza dough at room temperature

2 tablespoons basil infused oil (available in most supermarkets)

½ cup Marion's Marinara Sauce (page 164)

2 ounces whole milk mozzarella cheese, shredded (approximately ½ cup)

2 ounces asiago cheese, shredded

¼ cup Parmigiano-Reggiano cheese, grated

¼ cup Pecorino Romano cheese, grated on a Microplane®

2 large vine ripened tomatoes of any color, sliced ⅛ to ¼ inch thick, freshness is a must!

5 to 6 fresh basil leaves, torn

shaved Parmigiano-Reggiano – a few pieces for each tomato slice

additional small basil leaves for garnish

kosher salt and freshly ground black pepper

1 Roll, stretch and shape dough into an unrefined 12 by 14 inch rectangular or circular shape, according to basic directions, stretching it quite thin.

2 Brush both sides of dough with basil infused oil and place on a pizza peel or a large, rimless baking sheet that has been dusted with cornmeal.

3 Carefully lift dough and lay it on the preheated grill, turning center burner to low (see Grilled Pizza Primer.) Close grill lid and grill for 3 to 5 minutes or until bottom of crust is golden brown with darker grill marks. Remove from grill with tongs and place grilled side up on a flat baking sheet or pizza peel. Spread marinara sauce evenly on grilled side of dough.

4 Place mozzarella, asiago, Parmigiano-Reggiano and Pecorino Romano cheese in a small bowl and toss lightly to combine. Sprinkle cheese evenly over marinara sauce.

5 Arrange sliced tomatoes over top, being careful not to overlap them. Top each tomato with a few pieces of the shaved Parmigiano-Reggiano cheese.

6 Carefully slide pizza onto grill, leaving burner directly under pizza on low. Close lid and bake for 5 minutes. Check bottom of crust by lifting the edge with tongs. If it is browning too quickly, turn off burner under pizza and continue baking for 5 minutes.

7 Remove pizza from heat; scatter small basil leaves over top and season to taste with salt and pepper. Drizzle with a bit of good quality extra virgin olive oil if desired. Cut and serve immediately.

Sunny Southwestern Chicken Cobb Pizza

Bacon, avocado, chicken, tomato, and eggs diced and placed in perfectly aligned rows atop a bed of fresh greens...the Cobb Salad...one of our favorite foods for many years. My husband and I virtually lived on these salads during the days we were unpacking in Arizona after relocating from Connecticut. Once settled, I began to incorporate local ingredients and spices into our meals. "Could a Cobb Salad go southwestern?" I wondered – why not? I would like to think that even Bob Cobb would approve of this play on his incredible salad.

8 ounces chicken tenders or boneless skinless chicken breast

½ cup all-purpose flour

½ teaspoon kosher salt

¼ teaspoon freshly ground black pepper

¾ teaspoon chipotle chili powder divided

1 extra large egg, beaten with 1 tablespoon water

½ cup plain dry bread crumbs

4 tablespoons extra virgin olive oil, divided

2 tablespoons unsalted butter

4 ounces bacon, diced (3 to 4 slices)

8 to 9 ounces prepared pizza dough at room temperature

1 recipe Roasted Red Pepper Pesto (page 174)

2 ounces shredded pepper jack cheese – about ½ cup

2 ounces shredded Monterey Jack cheese – about ½ cup

½ cup red onion, cut into fine dice

10 cherry tomatoes, halved or quartered and drained on paper towels

1 heart romaine lettuce, sliced crosswise into ¼ inch strips

Avocado Ranch Dressing (recipe follows)

1 hardboiled egg, peeled and minced for garnish

Manchego cheese, shaved for garnish

1 If using chicken tenders, be sure they are of even thickness or follow directions for chicken breast halves. Place one chicken breast half into a plastic bag or between two pieces of plastic wrap and pound to ¼ inch thick; repeat with second piece. On a rimmed plate, mix flour with salt, pepper, and ¼ teaspoon chipotle chili powder. Place beaten egg into a shallow bowl; stir the remaining chipotle chili powder into the bread crumbs on another plate. To bread the chicken tenders or cutlets, dip each piece into flour mixture, shake off excess, and then dip into the egg, allowing excess to drip off. Press into bread crumbs to coat evenly. Place on a baking sheet and repeat with remaining pieces. Heat 2 tablespoons of the olive oil in a medium, heavy bottom sauté pan over medium-high heat; add butter and heat until butter foam subsides. Depending on the size of the pan, carefully place chicken tenders or one or both chicken cutlets into the pan. Cutlets should not overlap. Cook for approximately 2 to 3 minutes on the first side. Turn the cutlets and brown for 2 minutes longer to crisp the breading on the second side. Remove from pan, place on a plate and loosely cover with foil to keep warm for topping.

EXTREME TIME SAVER TIP: Use store bought breaded chicken tenders from deli or freezer section. Cook as directed.

2 Sauté bacon until all fat is rendered and bacon is lightly browned. Remove pan from heat and drain bacon on a paper towel lined plate. Set aside for topping.

3 Roll, stretch and shape dough into an unrefined circular or rectangular shape approximately 12 by 14 inches according to basic directions. Brush both sides of dough with 2 tablespoons of the olive oil and place on a large, rimless baking sheet or pizza peel that has been dusted with cornmeal. Carefully lift dough and lay it on the preheated grill (see Grilled Pizza Primer.) Close grill lid and grill for 3 to 5 minutes or until bottom of crust is golden brown with darker grill marks. Remove from grill with tongs and place grilled side up on a flat baking sheet or pizza peel.

4 Spread crust with a thin layer of roasted red pepper pesto; combine pepper jack and Monterey Jack cheese and sprinkle half of the mixture over the pesto.

5 Slice chicken tenders crosswise into ¼ inch pieces. If using cutlets, slice into ½ inch strips. Depending on size of cutlet, you might choose to cut each strip in half horizontally. Be careful not to make the pieces so small that the breading drops off; arrange over cheese.

6 Top with diced onion and cherry tomatoes. Sprinkle remaining cheese over all.

7 Carefully slide pizza onto grill, turning burner directly under pizza to low. Close lid and bake for 5 minutes. Check bottom of crust by lifting the edge with tongs. If it is browning too quickly, turn off burner directly under pizza and continue baking for 5 to 7 minutes or until crust is golden and cheese is melted and bubbly.

8 While pizza is baking, toss romaine with enough of the avocado ranch dressing to lightly coat it. Remove pizza from grill and slice. Top with dressed romaine, sprinkle minced egg and diced bacon over greens and shave Manchego cheese over all. Season with salt and pepper if desired. Serve immediately.

Tip

Chipotle chili powder is made from ripe, smoke-dried jalapenos. It can have quite a kick, so unless you want your chicken smokin' hot, add only ¼ teaspoon to the breadcrumbs.

Avocado Ranch Dressing - Yield approximately 1½ cups

- **1 ripe Hass avocado, pitted**
- **1 tablespoon lime juice, freshly squeezed**
- **¼ cup mayonnaise (recommended brand – Hellmann's®)**
- **¼ cup sour cream**
- **5 tablespoons buttermilk**
- **½ teaspoon kosher salt**
- **½ teaspoon freshly ground black pepper**
- **½ teaspoon granulated sugar**
- **1 clove garlic, minced**
- **1 tablespoon minced red onion**
- **1 tablespoon fresh cilantro leaves, minced**

1 In a food processor, pulse flesh from avocado and lime juice 5 to 6 times, or until avocado looks mashed.

2 Add mayonnaise, sour cream and buttermilk; process to combine.

3 Add salt, pepper, sugar, garlic, red onion and cilantro; process until completely smooth.

4 Cover and refrigerate, allowing 30 minutes for flavors to blend. Store in refrigerator for up to one week.

Surgeon's Diversion Pizza

The minutes dragged on as the saline dripped methodically through my IV, rehydrating my body while I nervously awaited my orthopedic surgeon. Before long, he approached and, upon seeing him, I thought to myself, "This man is energy personified." Within a minute or two, Dr. Cheleuitte checked my chart, looked at my foot, reassured me, and was good to go; ready to return to the operating room. When he caught a glimpse of the book I was reading, I told him it was research for a pizza cookbook I was writing. Within seconds, he was at the side of my bed, elbows perched on the bed rail, talking about what he would consider to be the perfect pizza, weaving in details of his heritage and describing some of the amazing Mediterranean dishes his mother prepared. Within minutes he conjured up a pizza containing fresh figs, chicken, olive oil, almonds and lemon; no doubt a combination of foods he had enjoyed before. I imagined the sweetness of figs complimenting the seasoned chicken coupled with the added complexity from the crunchiness of the almonds all being brought together with a drizzle of fruity olive oil and a splash of fresh lemon juice. I was duly impressed with his ability to instantly and effortlessly create a pizza, a simple diversion from a surgeon's hectic and demanding schedule.

6 ounces cooked chicken thigh meat, shredded or thinly sliced (recipe follows)

8 to 9 ounces prepared pizza dough at room temperature

2 tablespoons extra virgin olive oil, plus more for drizzling

4 ounces crumbled goat cheese, divided (approximately 1 cup)

4 fresh figs, cut into quarters or 8 dried figs, thinly sliced on an angle

3 tablespoons sliced almonds, very lightly toasted

4 to 6 fresh basil leaves, chiffonade

freshly grated lemon zest

one squeeze fresh lemon juice

1 Roll, stretch and shape dough into an unrefined 10 to 12 inch circular or rectangular shape according to basic directions. Place dough on a pizza peel or on a rimless baking sheet that has been lightly dusted with cornmeal. Brush with extra virgin olive oil.

2 Sprinkle half of the goat cheese over dough and scatter shredded or diced chicken over all.

3 Arrange figs over chicken to within one half inch from edge and top with remaining cheese.

4 Scatter almonds over all and finish with a light drizzle of olive oil.

5 Bake on a preheated Pizza Grill or on a preheated pizza stone in a 500° F. oven, rotating pizza after four minutes to prevent sticking. Bake for 10 to 12 minutes or until crust is firm and golden and ingredients are warmed through.

6 Remove from heat and immediately distribute basil chiffonade over pizza. Grate fresh lemon zest to taste over top; finish with a squeeze of fresh lemon juice and a drizzle of extra virgin olive oil.

continued on next page...

Mediterranean Chicken Thighs – Yield 2 thighs

2 chicken thighs, bone in and skin on

2 tablespoons freshly squeezed lemon juice (approximately ½ lemon)

2 tablespoons extra virgin olive oil

kosher salt and freshly ground black pepper to taste

¼ teaspoon dried parsley flakes

1 Squeeze lemon juice over chicken thighs and drizzle evenly with olive oil.

2 Season both sides of each thigh with kosher salt and black pepper to taste.

3 Sprinkle with dried parsley flakes.

4 Bake in a preheated 400° F. oven for 20 to 25 minutes or until just cooked through. Alternatively, the thighs can be grilled over medium heat for 10 to 12 minutes per side.

5 Remove skin and discard. Remove meat from bones and slice, shred or dice it. Reserve for pizza.

HELPFUL HINT: *Double or triple this recipe, serve for dinner with a fruity rice pilaf; use left over chicken for your pizza.*

Sweet Meets Heat Pizza

Upon returning from a trip to New Orleans, my husband Charlie could not stop talking about food he enjoyed while there. He went on and on about the incredible beignets he had each morning and about the highly spiced jambalaya teeming with fresh seafood, red beans and rice that he enjoyed for dinner. Then, out of nowhere came his discourse about loving the combination of sweet potatoes with andouille sausage. That sounded intriguing so I asked him to describe the dish he had that contained both the sausage and sweet potatoes. He looked puzzled by my question and said, "I never had anything like that, I just thought they would be good together." I had to laugh. Giving him the benefit of my doubt, I experimented with these ingredients and the result was simply delightful. Sweet potatoes and andouille sausages converge upon a peachy base. It is love at first sight, a perfect marriage of sweet and heat. They exchange rings (shallot) and are showered, not with confetti, but with shreds of rich, nutty fontina cheese. What a wedding!

1 sweet potato, about 8 ounces, peeled

¼ cup extra virgin olive oil, divided

kosher salt and freshly ground black pepper

8 to 9 ounces prepared pizza dough at room temperature

2 tablespoons fresh thyme leaves, chopped

⅛ teaspoon crushed red pepper flakes, plus more for finishing

8 ounces Andouille sausage

½ cup peach preserves or peach chutney for less sweetness

4 ounces whole milk mozzarella, shredded

1 large shallot, about 3 ounces, thinly sliced

2 to 4 ounces fontina cheese, shredded

red chili pepper oil, to taste

1. Slice sweet potato crosswise on a deep angle into ¼ inch slices. Brush with 2 tablespoons olive oil and season with kosher salt and pepper. Over indirect heat, grill slices for 8 to 10 minutes per side, or until softened and well marked. Potato slices can be baked on a baking sheet in a preheated 350° F. oven for about 20 minutes, turning once. Cover loosely with plastic wrap and set aside for topping.
2. Knead thyme leaves and red pepper flakes (if desired) into pizza dough; set aside.
3. Heat a medium skillet over medium-high heat. Remove sausage meat from links if necessary; add to the pan and cook, breaking meat apart for about 5 to 7 minutes or until sausage is cooked through and lightly browned. Drain fat and set sausage aside for topping.
4. Roll, stretch and shape dough into an unrefined 12 by 14 inch rectangular or a circular shape according to basic directions. Brush dough with remaining 2 tablespoons of olive oil. Spread peach preserves evenly over dough, leaving a ½ inch border. Sprinkle mozzarella cheese over preserves.
5. Arrange sweet potato slices over pizza, creating a pattern if desired. Scatter crumbled andouille over and around the potatoes. Roughly separate shallot into rings and distribute over pizza. Top with fontina cheese, using more or less as desired.
6. Bake on a preheated Pizza Grill or on a preheated pizza stone in a 500° F. oven, rotating pizza after 4 minutes to prevent sticking. Bake for 10 to 12 minutes or until crust is firm and golden, top is lightly browned and cheese is bubbly.
7. Remove from heat and, if desired, drizzle with chili pepper oil and sprinkle on a pinch of red pepper flakes.
8. Cut and serve immediately.

Tilly's Dream Pizza

After consuming a huge Christmas dinner, my nephew Tilly, a.k.a. Philip, fell into a sound sleep while stretched out on the living room floor. Upon awakening he remained on the floor, slowly turning his head from side to side, repeating, "I had a dream, I had a dream." Are you okay, Tilly, I said quietly. "O yea," he answered, "I had a dream about a meatloaf pizza and it was so damn good." The pizza or the dream, I queried. "The pizza!" So, there it was and here it is – Tilly's Dream Pizza.

- **6 ounces Momma's Meatloaf, cut into ¼ inch slices (page 172)**
- **½ to 1 cup Garlic Mashed Potatoes (recipe follows)**
- **8 to 9 ounces prepared pizza dough at room temperature**
- **1 tablespoon extra virgin olive oil**
- **⅓ to ½ cup barbecue sauce**
- **2 ounces cheddar cheese, shredded**
- **2 ounces muenster cheese, shredded**
- **3 to 4 scallions, white and light green parts sliced on an angle**

1. Roll, stretch and shape dough into an unrefined 12 by 14 inch rectangular or circular shape according to basic directions. Brush with olive oil.
2. Spread a thin coat of barbecue sauce evenly over dough, leaving a ½ inch border. Sprinkle cheddar cheese over sauce.
3. Arrange slices of meatloaf over cheese, roughly breaking them apart as you place them. Dot with spoonsful of the mashed potato mixture, nestling small mounds among the meatloaf. Sprinkle with the muenster cheese and scatter scallions over all.
4. Bake on a preheated Pizza Grill or on a preheated pizza stone in a 500° F. oven for 10 to 12 minutes or until potatoes are puffed and golden and cheese is bubbly. Rotate pizza after first 4 minutes to prevent sticking.
5. Remove from heat; drizzle with additional barbecue sauce if desired. Cut and serve immediately.

Garlic Mashed Potatoes

- **1 pound Yukon Gold potatoes, peeled and cut into large dice**
- **3 tablespoons unsalted butter, divided**
- **2 large cloves garlic, minced**
- **⅛ teaspoon freshly ground black pepper**
- **½ teaspoon kosher salt**
- **4 to 5 tablespoons whole milk or cream, hot**

1. In a small skillet over medium heat, melt 2 tablespoons of the butter. Add garlic, stir and cook at a very slow simmer just until garlic begins to turn golden. Remove from heat and set aside while potatoes cook.
2. Place potatoes in a medium saucepan and cover with water. Add ½ teaspoon salt to the water and bring to a boil. Lower heat and cook potatoes at a simmer for about 15 minutes or until tender when pierced with a fork. Drain potatoes and return to pot. Smash slightly with a potato masher, drizzle garlic butter over potatoes and season with salt and pepper. Add remaining tablespoon of butter and a few tablespoons of the milk or cream. Mash until smooth, adding more milk or cream if potatoes seem dry. The consistency should resemble that of thick sour cream. Set aside approximately one cup for topping.

Uncle John's 'shrooms Pizza

Mmm, 'shrooms! You could always count on hearing that from our dear friend John M. as he looked over what was cooking on the stove. Whenever he and Peg brought the boys down for a visit, there would be plenty of food and I would be sure to make John's favorite because it was such a pleasure to watch him savor each garlic infused 'shroom. Leave the small mushrooms whole if you prefer them the way John did. Enjoy!

2 tablespoons fresh thyme leaves, chopped plus more for garnish

½ cup Parmigiano-Reggiano cheese, freshly grated on a Microplane®; divided

8 to 9 ounces prepared pizza dough at room temperature

2 tablespoons unsalted butter

4 to 6 ounces baby portabella mushrooms

6 to 8 ounces white button mushrooms

pinch kosher salt

2 tablespoons extra virgin olive oil

¼ cup Roasted Garlic Paste (page 170)

4 ounces whole milk mozzarella cheese, shredded (approximately 1 cup)

4 ounces asiago cheese, shredded

freshly ground black pepper to taste

pinch sea salt

1. Knead chopped thyme leaves and ¼ cup of the Parmigiano-Reggiano cheese into the pizza dough. Set aside.
2. Brush mushrooms with a dry pastry brush to clean; trim stems and cut into ¼ inch thick slices. Heat 2 tablespoons of the oil in a large sauté pan over medium-high heat. When oil is hot, add butter and heat until butter foams. When foam subsides, add mushrooms and a pinch of kosher salt. Cook for a few minutes undisturbed, then stir occasionally and cook until mushrooms are lightly browned, about 8 to 10 minutes. Set aside to cool for topping. If using larger quantity of mushrooms, use one additional tablespoon of olive oil.
3. Roll, stretch and shape dough into an unrefined 12 to 14 inch circular or rectangular shape according to basic directions. Mix remaining 2 tablespoons of olive oil and the garlic paste; spread evenly over dough.
4. In a small bowl, combine remaining ¼ cup Parmigiano-Reggiano cheese, mozzarella and asiago cheese. Sprinkle one half the mixed cheeses over garlic paste on dough. Evenly distribute sautéed mushrooms over cheese. Top with remaining cheese mixture.
5. Bake on a preheated Pizza Grill or on a preheated pizza stone in 500° F. oven, rotating after 4 minutes to prevent sticking. Bake for 10 minutes, or until crust is firm and golden and cheese is bubbly.
6. Remove from heat and season with a pinch of sea salt and freshly ground black pepper to taste. Scatter tiny leaves from 2 to 3 sprigs of fresh thyme over all.

Cut and serve immediately.

The best way I have of rating this pizza is to quote my brother-in-law Ervin, a gifted surgeon, IVF doctor and man of very few words. After consuming several pieces of the 'shrooms pizza, he looked up and with a wide grin on his face said, "It's a keeper!" Now that's an endorsement. Oh, did I mention that Ervin does not like mushrooms?

Zucchini Zippady Doo-Dah Pizzah

A summer never went by that my dear friend Karen didn't gift me with an abundance of zucchini squash from her garden. She and her husband John used to grow tomatoes and zucchini – the perfect combination for a summer stew. Each time I prepared the fresh zucchini, I would adjust the ingredients or add something new; sometimes more garlic, more basil, chick peas, and even cooked macaroni. By summer's end, there was no end to what I could do with those blessed zucchini! This pizza contains ingredients that at one time or another found their way into my summer zucchini stew. The zip in this doo-dah pizza has many sources. The crushed red pepper in the crust, the arrabbiata sauce, the peppered zucchini slices and the rings of pepperoncini scattered about all add to the 'zip factor'. Once you taste this pizza, you will find yourself singing..."My, oh my, what a wonderful day!"

2 tablespoons freshly squeezed lemon juice

¼ teaspoon kosher salt

¾ teaspoon crushed red pepper flakes, divided

1 tablespoon fresh basil leaves, chopped

1 clove garlic, minced

⅛ teaspoon freshly ground black pepper

5 tablespoons extra virgin olive oil, divided

3 medium zucchini squash, approximately 1 pound

2 tablespoons lemon zest, divided

8 to 9 ounces prepared pizza dough at room temperature

⅓ cup Simple Arrabbiata Sauce (recipe follows) Use up to ½ cup if desired

4 ounces whole milk mozzarella, shredded (approximately 1 cup)

2 ounces Prosciutto di Parma, very thinly sliced

1 to 2 pepperoncini, drained, seeded and cut into ⅛ inch rings

2 tablespoons pine nuts

1 ounce Parmigiano-Reggiano cheese, freshly grated on a Microplane® plus additional for garnish

1 In a medium bowl, make vinaigrette by combining 2 tablespoons lemon juice, ¼ teaspoon kosher salt, ¼ teaspoon of the red pepper flakes, basil, garlic and ⅛ teaspoon freshly ground black pepper in a small bowl. Wisk in 4 tablespoons of the olive oil. Let flavors blend while preparing the zucchini. Wash and dry zucchini; cut off both ends then cut zucchini lengthwise into very thin slices. A mandolin slicer works well here. Gently toss zucchini slices with the lemon vinaigrette. Grill zucchini slices over medium-high heat for approximately 2 to 3 minutes per side or until they have grill marks and are slightly softened. Set aside for topping.

2 Knead remaining ½ teaspoon of the crushed red pepper flakes and 1 tablespoon of the lemon zest into the pizza dough. Roll, stretch and shape dough into an unrefined circular or rectangular shape approximately 12 by 14 inches, according to basic directions. Leaving a ½ inch border spread arrabbiata sauce evenly over dough and scatter mozzarella over sauce.

3 Separate prosciutto ribbons somewhat as you scatter them over the cheese. Top with grilled zucchini slices; do not lay the zucchini slices flat on the pizza, instead lift and twist them a bit to give them a ruffled look. Scatter pepperoncini rings and pine nuts over zucchini and top all with grated Parmigiano-Reggiano cheese.

4 Bake on a preheated Pizza Grill or on a preheated pizza stone in a 500° F. oven, rotating pizza after 4 minutes to prevent sticking. Bake for 10 to 12 minutes or until crust is firm and golden, zucchini slices are lightly browned and cheese is melted.

5 Remove from heat and garnish with remaining 1 tablespoon of lemon zest. Shave Parmigiano-Reggiano with a vegetable peeler over top of pizza as desired and drizzle with remaining tablespoon of olive oil. Cut and serve.

Simple Arrabbiata Sauce

- **2 tablespoons extra virgin olive oil**
- **2 cloves garlic, minced**
- **½ teaspoon crushed red pepper flakes**
- **1 (32 ounce) jar marinara or tomato-basil spaghetti sauce**

1. Heat olive oil in a medium saucepan over medium heat; add garlic and red pepper flakes. Sauté for 1 to 2 minutes, being careful not to burn the garlic.
2. Add sauce, heat through and simmer for 7 to 10 minutes to blend flavors.
3. Cool before using on pizza.

Helpful Hint: *You can use prepared arrabbiata sauce in place of Simple Arrabiata Sauce – makes life a lot easier!*

Recommended: Rao's® Arrabbiata Sauce

Tip

Tightly roll prosciutto slices lengthwise like a cigar then cut crosswise at ¼ inch intervals into thin ribbons. Toss gently to separate 'ribbons'.

Prepping Pizza

Heading to Grill

Julia
Proud Pizza Maker

Kids' Pizzas

Welcome to the wonderful world of your child's imagination. The recipes in this section are totally kid friendly in that the children can roll, stretch and shape their own dough, spread sauces, choose and arrange their own toppings and take great pride in their accomplishment when the finished product comes out of the oven or off the grill. Depending on your child's age, you will need to prepare some of the toppings in advance; but assembling the pizzas can be done with little or no assistance from the grown ups.

Although our granddaughter Julia just celebrated her sixth birthday, she can stretch and shape pizza dough better than many of the adults I know. On a recent visit to us in Arizona, she made her own pizzas for dinner. There was flour everywhere – on the board, the surrounding counter and even on her forehead. She was so intensely involved; you could see the concentration on her little face as she carefully listened to my instructions for rolling and stretching her dough. She mastered the task in record time and moved on to assembling two small pizzas to her exact specifications. Julia has always loved helping in the kitchen; and it is my belief that, with a little encouragement, most children can develop a true love for cooking. What fun we had that evening.

Please be sure to keep in mind that you need not be limited by the recipes in this section; rather, use them as a springboard for your child's imagination. You might be pleasantly surprised – children are so creative.

Quesadilla-No ~ Pizza-Sí

How many times did you hear, "Don't play with your food" when you were growing up? Parents are so serious sometimes. My mother certainly was. As I remember, we were not allowed to laugh at the dinner table because we said grace before meals and my mother thought it was somehow disrespectful. This rule might not have been that unreasonable for some, but it was highly problematic for me – the family clown! Not only did I live to make people laugh, I could not stop myself from laughing once I started. Thanks to my sister Elaine, who got me going every night, I was sent away from the dinner table more times than I can count. So, I am hereby giving all kids and kids at heart permission to play while creating these pizzas and laugh while eating them – enjoy the process!

8 to 9 ounces prepared pizza dough at room temperature

2 tablespoons extra virgin olive oil

½ cup base sauce

4 ounces cheese, shredded and divided (approximately 1 to 1½ cups)

1 cup toppings

1. Roll, stretch and shape dough into an unrefined 10 to 12 inch rectangular or circular shape according to basic directions.
2. Brush dough with olive oil.
3. Spread enough sauce on dough to lightly cover with an even layer.
4. Sprinkle one half the cheese over base sauce and scatter topping or combination of toppings over cheese. Top with remaining cheese.
5. Bake on a preheated Pizza Grill or on a preheated pizza stone in a 500o F. oven for 10 to 12 minutes or until crust is firm and golden and cheese is bubbly. Rotate pizza after first 4 minutes to prevent sticking.
6. Remove from heat, cool for one minute then cut and serve.

Base Sauce

Spanish Sofrito **

Pizza Sauce

Salsa – tomato or pineapple

Tomato Sauce (Hunt's®)

Mushroom Tapenade **

Cilantro Pesto **

Cheese

Manchego

Cheddar

Monterey Jack

Jalapeno Jack

Asadero

Mexican 5 blend

Asiago

Mozzarella

Cotija

Toppings

Shredded cooked chicken

Cooked crumbled chorizo

Shrimp, halved lengthwise

Roasted corn kernels

Onion, sliced or chopped

Bell peppers, thinly sliced

Zucchini matchsticks

Mushrooms, sliced

Fresh pineapple, small diced

Spanish olives, halved or sliced

Tip

Divide the dough into four equal parts to make individual pizzas.

Choose one base sauce, one or two cheeses (totaling 1½ cups) and a few toppings. Be sure not to overload your pizza with toppings or it will remain soggy in the center.

**See Sassy Sauces and Tasty Topping

Beanie Wiener Pizza

When our son and daughter were young, we would occasionally allow them to choose a restaurant destination for dinner. They usually chose Lenders Bagel Restaurant. Jen, so she could watch the bagels floating in huge vats of boiling water; Matt, because they served 'Franks and Beans' – a meal he could ***never*** *get at home! Matt ate almost as many franks and beans as all his other "acceptable food list" foods combined. He still loves them to this day.*

⅓ cup ketchup – recommended brand - Heinz®

1 tablespoon mustard

8 to 9 ounces prepared pizza dough at room temperature

2 ounces whole milk mozzarella cheese, shredded

2 ounces white cheddar cheese, shredded

½ cup canned baked beans, drained of excess liquid

4 ounces hot dogs, cut crosswise into ¼ inch slices

2 to 3 slices bacon, cooked, drained and crumbled

1. Place ketchup and mustard in a small bowl and stir to combine; set aside.
2. Roll, stretch and shape dough into an unrefined 10 to 12 inch circular or rectangular shape according to basic directions.
3. Spread ketchup mixture evenly over dough, leaving a one half inch border.
4. Combine mozzarella and cheddar cheese and sprinkle one half of the mixture over the ketchup base.
5. Spoon beans evenly around pizza then scatter hot dog slices over beans. Top with remaining cheese mixture.
6. Bake on a preheated Pizza Grill or on a preheated pizza stone in a 500° F. oven for 10 to 12 minutes or until crust is firm and golden and cheese is bubbly. Rotate pizza after first 4 minutes to prevent sticking.
7. Remove from heat and top with crumbled bacon; cool for one to two minutes. Cut and serve.

Tip

If serving this pizza to younger children, you may choose to cut the hotdogs into small dice. You can eliminate the cheddar cheese, using 4 ounces of mozzarella in its place. The taste of this pizza can be further simplified by eliminating the bacon garnish.

Chicken Pot 'Pie'zza

The brothers Faherty – Kyle, Nolan and Griffin love spending time together. Whether assembling Legos, playing hockey or fighting imaginary bad guys, when you see one, you know that the others will be close at hand. Another thing the boys love is being called to one of their favorite dinners, chicken pot pies. One evening the boys sat down to eat and as usual had trouble quieting themselves; then the pot pies appeared. Heads went down; a silence enveloped them as they hungrily spooned up the warm chicken and vegetable mixture. Then, quite out of the blue, Griffin, the youngest brother spoke up. "Mommy" he said, "I really like the chicken, the pot and the pie, but not the peas." Mommy had to laugh knowing that at only three years old, little Griff had a mind of his own and no problem verbalizing his likes and dislikes. I'm still not sure what it is about chicken pot pie that is irresistibly comforting to kids and adults alike. Could it be the bubbling sauce in which the mixture of tasty vegetables and chicken is nestled – or perhaps it is just the love with which the pot pie is assembled, baked and served? For whatever reason, pot pies are loved by many. So, forget the pot, forget the peas if you are like Griffin, stretch some dough and enjoy your Chicken 'Not' Pie!

---

1 carrot, peeled and cut crosswise into ¼ inch slices (⅓ cup)

2 small red potatoes, peeled and cut into ¼ inch dice

8 ounces condensed cream of chicken soup – recommended brand - Campbell's®

¼ teaspoon kosher salt

⅛ teaspoon freshly ground black pepper

¼ teaspoon sweet paprika

4 ounces whole milk mozzarella, shredded (1 cup)

¼ cup frozen peas, thawed

¼ cup frozen corn kernels, thawed

8 to 9 ounces prepared pizza dough at room temperature

2 tablespoons extra virgin olive oil

1 cup cooked chicken cubes (approximately 5 to 6 ounces)

2 ounces fontina cheese, shredded

1 Place carrot slices and diced potatoes in a medium saucepan. Cover with water and bring to a boil; lower heat and simmer for about 7 minutes or until vegetables are just tender when pierced with a fork. Drain, cover and set aside.

2 In a medium bowl, combine cream of chicken soup, salt, pepper, paprika and mozzarella cheese, remove ½ cup of the mixture and set the remainder aside.

3 Place cooked carrots and potatoes and the peas and corn in a bowl and toss with the ½ cup of reserved soup/cheese mixture. Set aside for topping.

4 Roll, stretch and shape dough into an unrefined 10 by 12 inch rectangular or circular shape according to basic directions. Brush both sides of dough with the olive oil and place on a large, rimless baking sheet or pizza peel that has been lightly dusted with cornmeal. Carefully lift dough and lay it on the preheated grill (see Grilled Pizza Primer.) Close grill lid and grill for 3 to 5 minutes or until bottom of crust is golden brown with darker grill marks. Remove from grill with tongs and place grilled side up on a flat baking sheet or pizza peel.

5 Spread soup/cheese mixture evenly over grilled side of dough to within ½ inch from edge. Carefully slide pizza onto grill, turning burner directly under pizza to low. Close lid and bake for 3 to 4 minutes, or until soup and cheese begin to melt. Using tongs, carefully remove pizza to a pizza peel. Close grill lid.

6 Quickly scatter chicken cubes and vegetable mixture over soup/cheese layer. Top all with fontina cheese. Turn off burner directly under pizza. Return to grill and bake for 5 to 7 minutes longer or until crust is firm, topping is bubbling and cheese is melted.

7 Remove from grill and season with freshly ground black pepper.

Doggone Delicious Pizza

"In the old days" when my two children were growing up, they ate more hot dogs than I can count. Those were the days of serving them hotdogs cut into hunks, not being aware of the major choking hazard involved in that practice. What did we know...we also let them use Lawn Darts! Most kids love hot dogs and helping in the kitchen. If you allow the children to arrange the hot dog slices and squiggle on the ketchup, they may even come up with other toppings they want to include.

- **8 to 9 ounces prepared pizza dough at room temperature**
- **⅓ cup tomato sauce – recommended brand – Hunt's®**
- **4 ounces cheddar cheese, shredded and divided**
- **4 ounces hotdogs, cut crosswise into ¼ inch slices**
- **¼ cup chopped kosher baby dill pickles or sweet gherkin pickles**
- **¼ cup ketchup, transferred to a squirt bottle**

1. Roll, stretch and shape dough into a 10 to 12 inch circular or rectangular shape according to basic directions. Spread tomato sauce evenly over dough.
2. Sprinkle one half the cheddar cheese over the sauce and place hot dog slices over the cheese. Have the kids make a few squiggles with the ketchup squirt bottle and top with remaining cheese.
3. Bake on a preheated Pizza Grill or on a preheated pizza stone in a 500° F. oven, rotating after 4 minutes to prevent sticking. Bake for 10 to 12 minutes or until crust is firm and golden and cheese is bubbly.
4. Remove from heat and top with chopped pickles and a few more squirts of ketchup. It is fun for older children to write or print their names, draw flowers, or balloons; the possibilities are endless. Allow pizza to set for 3 to 4 minutes before cutting.

Tip

If serving this pizza to younger children, you may choose to cut the hotdogs into small dice.

Going Bananas Pizza

Kids love to act goofy, monkey around or just go bananas – all in fun, of course. Many children I know also love peanut butter and banana sandwiches. So I thought, why not combine the behavior and the food to create a goofy pizza that they can have a ball making and have great fun eating as well?

½ cup apple juice

¼ cup raisins

½ cup peanut butter, chunky style

2 tablespoons

8 to 9 ounces

2 tablespoons honey, plus more in a squirt bottle for finishing

prepared pizza dough at room temperature

walnut oil

2 small bananas, ripe but firm, cut into ⅛ inch slices

Chocolate sprinkles and/or chopped roasted peanuts

1 In a small saucepan, bring apple juice to a boil. Add raisins adjust heat to a slow simmer for about 15 to 20 minutes or until raisins are plumped. Drain and set aside for topping.

2 Combine peanut butter and honey in a small bowl and set aside.

3 Roll, stretch and shape dough into an unrefined 10 to 12 inch circular or rectangular shape according to basic directions. Brush both sides of dough with the walnut oil and place on a large, rimless baking sheet or pizza peel that has been dusted with cornmeal. Carefully lift dough and lay it on the preheated grill (see Grilled Pizza Primer.) Close grill lid and grill for 3 to 5 minutes or until bottom of crust is golden brown with darker grill marks. Flip crust and continue to cook for 3 to 5 minutes longer or until golden and nicely marked. Remove from grill with tongs and place on a pizza peel or rimless cookie sheet.

4 Immediately spread peanut butter and honey mixture evenly to within one half inch from edge of crust while crust is still warm.

5 Top with banana slices and scatter raisins over all. You can pop it back on the grill for a minute or go ahead and finish it with a drizzle of honey and chocolate sprinkles/chopped peanuts as desired.

VARIATION:

Eliminate finishing honey drizzle and spoon small dollops of marshmallow crème randomly over top of pizza. For this variation, I suggest putting finished pizza back on the grill for a minute or two to melt the marshmallow crème.

Tip

Whole wheat dough also works well for this pizza.

Julia's Barnyard Pizza

Even before our granddaughter Julia was able to walk; her love for all animals was evident. We have pictures of her when she was less than 6 months old, sitting in a box with her grandma Bubbie's dog who was giving birth to a litter of puppies at the time. The look on her face was one of pure love – she was at one with those pups! In addition to the family pets, a German wire-haired dog named Ophelia and a really fat cat named Smithers, she is the proud "mother" of 5 chickens, 5 ducks, 2 guinea pigs and 2 rabbits, all of which she lovingly cares for and feeds. She takes after her grandma Bubbie who loves all animals and has taught Julia about the responsibility of having pets. I still cringe when I think of the day that Julia, who was about three years old, was showing me how she feeds her guinea pigs. Before I knew what she was doing, she had the cage open; guinea pig cradled in both her hands and was stretching her arms up toward me, asking me if I wanted to hold him. Well, my daughter-in-law Kim probably noticed the blood drain from my face as I fumbled for a reason to say no. "Ammie Lin can see him better if I hold him," Kim said. We laugh about it now, but I didn't think it was funny at the time. I love dogs, but I keep any other creatures at arm's length, not really understanding my unrealistic fears. I read stories to Julia about animals, we sing songs together about animals, but that's as far as I can go with it. She is 5 years old now and I can still see her as a little bit of a thing singing "Old MacDonald"....she knew every animal sound before she could even put a sentence together. While you are preparing this pizza with your children, encourage them to sing a few verses of that wonderful old song being sure to sing about the toppings - with an oink, oink here and a cluck, cluck there....E-I-E-I-O!!!

- **6 breakfast sausage links (not brown and serve)**
- **1 tablespoon canola or other vegetable oil**
- **2 tablespoons unsalted butter**
- **2 cups frozen shredded hash brown potatoes – like Ore-Ida Country Style®**
- **8 to 9 ounces prepared pizza dough at room temperature**
- **⅓ cup tomato sauce, recommended brand – Hunt's®**
- **4 ounces cheddar cheese, shredded and divided**
- **4 medium to large eggs**
- **kosher salt, to taste**
- **freshly ground black pepper, to taste**
- **ketchup in a squirt bottle**

1. Brown sausage links according to package directions, leaving them just a bit undercooked. Drain on a paper towel lined plate until cool enough to handle; cut crosswise into ¼ inch slices and set aside.

2. In a medium sauté pan, warm oil over medium-high heat; add butter and heat until butter melts and foam subsides. Add hash browns to the pan and cook, covered for 3 to 5 minutes. Uncover, stir and cook for 3 to 5 minutes longer, or until potatoes are just beginning to brown. Remove pan from heat. Residual heat from pan will keep potatoes warm while you are assembling your pizza.

3. Roll, stretch and shape dough into a 10 to 12 inch circular shape according to basic directions. Spread tomato sauce evenly over dough to within ½ inch from edge and sprinkle with half the cheese.

4. Using tongs, make four 'haystacks' by mounding one quarter of the pre-cooked hash browns on each quadrant of the pizza. With the back of a spoon, make a well in the top of each 'haystack'. Scatter sliced sausages over top of pizza around the potato haystacks. Carefully slip one egg into each well and sprinkle with remainder of the cheese. [Alternatively, sauté eggs in butter until set to your liking and place one in each well on top of baked pizza.]

5. Bake on a preheated Pizza Grill or on a preheated pizza stone in a 500° F. oven for 10 to 12 minutes or until crust is firm and golden, cheese is melted and eggs are set to your liking.

6 Remove from heat and season with salt and black pepper to taste. Cut into four equal slices, making sure there is one whole egg on each slice. Allow each child to 'decorate' his/her own piece with the ketchup, squirting it on each slice as desired.

HELPFUL HINT: *If making this pizza for children, cook eggs until set through then you can cut the pizza into smaller, easier to manage pieces. If you prefer your eggs soft set, I suggest using a knife and fork when consuming your pizza or you may end up with warm egg yolk running down your arms...never a good thing!*

With a chick chick here...

Tip

To make individual pizzas, divide dough into four equal pieces. Roll, stretch and shape into four circles according to basic directions. Follow directions above, dividing all ingredients equally among the four pizzas.

Crack each egg separately into a small cup before slipping onto the pizza.

Mags and Eli's Hawaiian Pizza

Eli and Mags (Margaux) love to visit Auntie Linda in Arizona for two reasons – they are allowed to make their own pizzas and then attend Auntie Linda and Uncle Charlie's annual anything goes, make your own sundae party. What a wonderful treat to watch this brother and sister duo debating serious issues such as thick or thin crust, sauce or no sauce, whether to place pineapple on pizza before or after ham, who has the best design and spacing of ingredients...on and on. It is quite comical to witness this as little hands busy themselves assembling their own perfect pizzas. Now, on to the Sundae Party!

- **8 to 9 ounces prepared pizza dough at room temperature**
- **2 tablespoons extra virgin olive oil**
- **⅓ cup Marion's Marinara Sauce; if sauce is desired (page 164)**
- **1½ cups shredded whole milk mozzarella cheese, divided**
- **3 to 4 slices fresh pineapple, peeled, cored and cut into ¼ to ½ inch dice**
- **1 (4 ounce) ham slice cut into ¼ to ½ inch dice**

1. Roll, stretch and shape dough into an unrefined 12 to 14 inch circular shape according to basic directions. Place on a pizza peel or rimless baking sheet that has been dusted with cornmeal; brush with extra virgin olive oil.
2. If you are using the marinara sauce, spread it evenly over the dough at this point.
3. Sprinkle half the cheese over dough or over sauce topped dough.
4. Top with diced pineapple and diced ham; sprinkle remaining cheese over all.
5. Bake on a preheated Pizza Grill or on a preheated pizza stone in a 500° F. oven, rotating after four minutes to prevent sticking. Bake for 10 minutes or until crust is firm and golden and cheese is bubbly.

Tip

To make individual pizzas, divide dough in half and shape each piece into a 6 to 8 inch circle or anything resembling a circle. Brush each circle with 1 tablespoon of olive oil. For each pizza, use ½ the amount of sauce and ¼ of the shredded cheese in steps 2 and 3. Top each pizza with half of the pineapple and half of the ham, then sprinkle ¼ of the remaining cheese over each pizza. Bake pizzas as in step 5 above, checking for doneness after 7 – 8 minutes.

Nick's No Nonsense Pizza

Having initially been diagnosed with cancer at the tender age of three and one half years, Nick, at age seven, was no stranger to pain and suffering. Yet, through it all, he never, ever complained. Nick loved life and enjoyed the simple pleasures derived from playing his guitar and riding his motorcycles, to mastering the latest video games available. But he mostly loved being with his family and friends of all ages. Nick's dad taught him how to make pizza and he greatly enjoyed making it often with his Auntie Em. His very favorite pizza was quite simple – fresh dough topped with sauce, mozzarella cheese and drizzled with olive oil. He was very particular about the way in which this pizza was made. Nick would tell Auntie Em to roll and roll the dough until it was quite thin and then would direct her not to bake it too close to the bottom of the oven. You see, Nick did not like burnt crust! Nick was the light of his Auntie Em's life and losing him this year left her with a huge hole in her heart. His strong spirit and memories of his love of the simple pleasures in life give her the courage to go on each day. When you make this pizza, be sure to take a lesson from Nick – do not complain about the things in life over which you have no control and please, don't burn the crust!

8 to 9 ounces prepared pizza dough at room temperature

1 tablespoon extra virgin olive oil, plus more for finishing

⅓ to ½ cup Marion's Marinara Sauce (page 164)

6 ounces whole milk mozzarella cheese, cut into ⅛ to ¼ inch slices, or shredded

½ teaspoon dried oregano (optional)

¼ cup freshly grated Parmigiano-Reggiano cheese

1. Roll, roll, and roll your dough until you have a 12 to 14 inch circular shape. Remember, Nick said the dough must be thin to be good. Place on a rimless baking sheet or a pizza peel that has been lightly dusted with cornmeal.
2. Brush dough with one tablespoon of olive oil. Spread marinara sauce in an even layer over the dough, using only enough to lightly coat the dough.
3. Arrange mozzarella cheese over the sauce and sprinkle oregano over all, if using.
4. Bake on a preheated Pizza Grill or on a preheated pizza stone in a 500° F. oven for 10 minutes, rotating pizza after 4 minutes to prevent sticking. Bake until crust is firm and golden and top is bubbly and lightly browned. This is the point at which Nick would give Auntie Em a stern warning not to let the crust burn.
5. Remove from the heat and immediately sprinkle with the Parmigiano-Reggiano cheese; drizzle with extra virgin olive oil to taste. Cut and serve immediately. Enjoy Nick's simple, no nonsense pizza.

Tip

You can use a good quality purchased sauce such as Rao's® Homemade Sauce in place of Marion's Marinara Sauce.

Pumpkin Patch Pizza

What could be more fun than watching children scuttle through a pumpkin patch in the fall – jumping over vines and stooping to find just the right pumpkin for carving or decorating? Time and again we witnessed the joy this brought to our granddaughter who would spend full days at her other grandmother's farm, The Berry Farm, in Connecticut simply wandering the fields. Continue the pumpkin patch fun at home; spread some pumpkin on pizza dough, let the children decorate it with their favorite fruits and veggies, bake and keep the party going!

- **¾ cup canned pumpkin puree**
- **½ cup mashed canned yams or baked sweet potato**
- **½ teaspoon ground cinnamon**
- **¼ teaspoon kosher salt**
- **freshly ground black pepper to taste**
- **8 to 9 ounces prepared pizza dough at room temperature**
- **2 tablespoons extra virgin olive oil**
- **4 ounces whole milk mozzarella cheese, shredded**
- **½ cup baby spinach leaves, washed and thoroughly dried**
- **1 apple, cored and thinly sliced**
- **2 ounces fontina cheese, cut into small cubes**
- **2 tablespoons roasted pumpkin seeds (salted)**

1. Layer four paper towels and place pumpkin puree in the center of the towels; spread out slightly with the back of a spoon. Top with a layer of four paper towels and gently press out excess moisture from pumpkin (pumpkin should be of spreadable consistency, not dry.) Quickly scrape pumpkin from paper towel and place in a small bowl; combine with mashed yams, cinnamon, salt and pepper. Set aside for topping.
2. Roll, stretch and shape dough into an unrefined 12 to 14 inch circular shape according to basic directions. Brush dough with olive oil.
3. Spread an even layer of the seasoned pumpkin mixture over dough. Top with shredded mozzarella cheese then scatter spinach leaves randomly over cheese. Arrange apple slices and fontina cheese cubes over all.
4. Bake on a preheated Pizza Grill or on a preheated pizza stone in a 500° F. oven, rotating after the first 4 minutes to prevent sticking. Bake for 10 to 12 minutes or until crust is firm and topping is lightly browned and bubbling.
5. Remove from heat and sprinkle with roasted pumpkin seeds. Cut then cool for a minute or two before serving.

Tip

To cube cheese, cut into ½ inch slices, stack a few slices at a time and cut lengthwise into ½ inch strips then crosswise, into ½ inch cubes.

Sloppy Jen's Pizza

Sloppy Joes were always a hit with my children, the juicier, the better. Little Jenny was always a sloppy eater. At the end of the day, I always knew what she had eaten by the telltale food stains on her clothes. She loved the evenings we had Sloppy Joes for dinner because it was one of the only times she could make it through the meal without being chastised for dropping food on herself. Today Jen has impeccable manners, having outgrown her sloppy eating, but not her eating of sloppy Joes...she still loves them. Use a fork and knife, if you must, when you eat your Sloppy Jen's Pizza.

1½ cup prepared Sloppy Joe Mix, at room temperature (recipe follows)

8 to 9 ounces prepared pizza dough at room temperature

2 tablespoons extra virgin olive oil

4 ounces cheddar cheese, shredded and divided (approximately 1 cup)

1 small green pepper, thinly sliced into rings

barbecue sauce for drizzling

1. Roll, stretch and shape dough into an unrefined 12 by 14 inch rectangular or circular shape according to basic directions. Place on a pizza peel or rimless baking sheet that has been dusted with cornmeal. Brush dough with olive oil and sprinkle with one half the cheese.
2. Spread Sloppy Joe Mix in an even layer to within ½ inch from edge of dough. Top with green pepper rings and remainder of cheese.
3. Bake on a preheated Pizza Grill or on a preheated pizza stone in a 500° F. oven for 10 to 12 minutes or until crust is firm and golden and cheese is bubbly. Rotate pizza after first 4 minutes to prevent sticking.
4. Remove from heat. If desired, drizzle with barbecue sauce to taste. Cut and serve with plenty of napkins!

Sloppy Joe Mix

- **1 tablespoon extra virgin olive oil**
- **1 pound ground beef**
- **1 small onion, chopped**
- **2 stalks celery, chopped**
- **1 small garlic clove, minced**
- **1 (8 ounce) can tomato sauce – recommended brand-Hunt's®**
- **1 tablespoon dark brown sugar***
- **¼ cup barbecue sauce, regular or spicy**
- **¼ cup ketchup – recommended brand - Heinz®**
- **½ teaspoon kosher salt**
- **¼ teaspoon freshly ground black pepper**
- **1 tablespoon Worcestershire® sauce**

1. Heat oil in a medium sauté pan over medium-high heat. Add ground beef and cook, breaking it apart with a spoon, for 5 minutes or until beef just loses its pink color.
2. Add onion, celery and garlic and cook for 5 minutes, stirring frequently. Drain off fat from pan.
3. In a small bowl, combine tomato sauce, brown sugar, barbecue sauce, ketchup, salt, pepper and Worcestershire® sauce; add to beef mixture. Stir to combine and slowly simmer for about 30 minutes or until sauce is reduced and thickened. Set aside to cool.

*Substitute one tablespoon light brown sugar and one teaspoon molasses for the dark brown sugar.

Dessert Pizzas

Having grown up in a rather large Italian family, I am no stranger to desserts. Each time our extended family gathered, be it for a birthday, baptism, graduation, wedding or a funeral, one or two of my aunts and cousins would haul out the huge trays of Italian cookies and pastries, and the fruit and cheese platters. The pleasure was not in consuming a huge dessert, it was mostly in having a little 'sweet' to go with that piping hot cup of coffee while bringing the visit to an end; at which time Auntie Ann would begin singing "The Party's Over." Everyone seemed to have his or her own favorite indulgence; mine was pignoli cookies, with cannoli running a close second. As a child, I would patiently wait my turn as the trays were passed, praying all the time that at least one pignoli cookie would survive as multiple hands rooted through biscotti, sfogliatelle (shfooy-adell') and cannoli, each person looking to connect with his or her own favorite.

No doubt, most of my older Italian relatives would never consider having pizza for dessert; an idea which also remains a foreign concept to many traditional pizza lovers who cannot think beyond sausage, pepperoni or mushroom pizza. I can assure you, though; once you taste the *Holy Cannoli Pizza* you will become a believer. A simple lemon tart pales in comparison to a piece of *Mary's Marvelous Lemon Tart Pizza* with its base of warm, creamy mascarpone cheese and topping of fresh raspberries scattered among dollops of cool, tangy lemon pudding. Whether you are in the mood for pie, a fresh fruit tart, or a gooey s'more you will find the perfect pizza with which to satisfy your desire; and don't forget to share the love!

Cinder-Ella's Coach Pizza

Ella is the fourth child born to our daughter's best friends, Jackie and Patrick. She is a most beautiful child and has been a true princess from birth. I say this because her three older siblings are brothers who consider her to ***be*** *a real princess. This pizza was created for her and since our Cinder-ella's godmother didn't have to turn a pumpkin into a coach to get her to the Royal Ball because her father, Sergeant Patrick F. will chauffeur her, we used the pumpkin to make a dessert pizza fit for a princess and her prince charming.*

¾ cup pumpkin puree, canned

¼ cup mascarpone cheese

2 tablespoons granulated sugar

¼ teaspoon vanilla extract

1 tablespoon crystallized ginger, finely chopped, plus extra for garnish

⅛ teaspoon ground cinnamon

⅛ teaspoon ground nutmeg

⅛ teaspoon ground ginger

¼ teaspoon salt

9 ounces Dessert or Plain Pizza Dough. Combine and knead into dough 2 tablespoons sugar and 1 teaspoon cinnamon.

2 tablespoons walnut oil

1 large banana, ripe but firm, sliced lengthwise then cut on an angle into ¼ to ½ inch thick slices

¼ cup butterscotch chips

¼ cup chocolate chips

¼ cup toasted walnut halves, chopped

1 Layer four paper towels and place pumpkin puree in the center of the towels; spread out slightly with the back of a spoon. Top with a layer of four paper towels and gently press out excess moisture from pumpkin (pumpkin should be of spreadable consistency, not dry.) Quickly scrape pumpkin from paper towel and place in a small bowl; add mascarpone, granulated sugar, vanilla, crystallized ginger, cinnamon, nutmeg, ground ginger and salt and stir to combine. Set aside for topping.

2 Roll, stretch and shape dough into an unrefined 12 by 14 inch rectangular shape according to basic directions. Brush both sides of dough with the walnut oil and place on a large, rimless baking sheet or pizza peel dusted with cornmeal. Carefully lift dough and lay it on the preheated grill; turn burner directly under pizza to low (see Grilled Pizza Primer.) Close grill lid and grill for 3 to 5 minutes or until bottom of crust is golden brown with darker grill marks. Remove from grill with tongs and place grilled side up on a flat baking sheet or pizza peel.

3 Evenly spread enough of the cheese/pumpkin mixture to form a thin coating over grilled side of dough, leaving a ½ inch border. Arrange banana slices over cheese and sprinkle on butterscotch and chocolate chips.

4 Carefully slide pizza onto grill, turning burner directly under pizza to low. Close lid and bake for 5 minutes. Check bottom of crust by lifting the edge with tongs. If it is browning too quickly, turn off burner directly under pizza and continue baking for 3 - 5 minutes or until crust is firm and golden, cheese is warmed and chips are slightly melted.

5 Remove from grill, sprinkle with chopped crystallized ginger to taste and with chopped walnuts. Cut into small squares and serve.

Tip

Eliminate butterscotch chips and substitute ¼ cup raisins that have been simmered for 20 minutes in ½ cup apple juice then drained.

Holy Cannoli Pizza

Oh, for the taste of a freshly made creamy, sweet, crunchy cannoli...I would do just about anything! I remember the day I was visiting our daughter in Connecticut. She lives only a few blocks from what is called the Italian section of town. On this particularly beautiful fall day, she was at work and I decided to go for a walk to get some exercise. As I put on my sneakers, I was feeling really good about choosing to do something that would be beneficial for my health. I walked for quite some time, taking in the beauty of the fall foliage and enjoying the cool, crisp air. Then, before I knew what was happening, I was within a few feet of Lucibella's Italian Bakery. Oh no, now what? Well, I thought, it would be foolish to be this close and not go in to purchase a cannoli!

8 to 9 ounces Dessert Pizza Dough at room temperature (page 25)

1 tablespoon granulated sugar

1 teaspoon ground cinnamon

1 tablespoon unsweetened cocoa powder

15 ounces whole milk ricotta cheese

¼ cup confectioner's sugar, plus more for dusting

½ teaspoon pure vanilla extract

1 teaspoon freshly grated orange zest, use a Microplane®

2 ounces bitter or bittersweet chocolate, chopped plus extra for garnish

2 tablespoons walnut (or other nut) oil

candied orange peel, chopped for garnish

2 tablespoons chopped pistachio nuts

1. Prepare Dessert Pizza Dough according to directions. In step 2, add granulated sugar, cinnamon, and cocoa powder to dry ingredients. Pulse 2 to 3 times to combine. Continue with recipe and set aside 8 to 9 ounces of the dough until ready to assemble the pizza. Refrigerate or freeze remaining dough in two pieces.

2. In a medium bowl, combine ricotta, confectioner's sugar, vanilla, orange zest and 2 ounces of the chopped chocolate. Stir until fully combined then refrigerate until ready to use. (This mixture can be made up to 24 hours in advance.)

3. Roll, stretch and shape dough into an unrefined rectangular shape approximately 12 by 14 inches according to basic directions. Brush both sides of the dough with walnut oil and place on a large rimless baking sheet or on a pizza peel that has been lightly dusted with cornmeal. Carefully lift dough and lay it on the pre-heated grill (see Grilled Pizza Primer.) Close grill lid and grill for 3 to 5 minutes or until bottom of crust is golden brown with darker grill marks. Turn over with tongs and grill for an additional 3 to 5 minutes until bottom is golden and crust is firm. Remove from grill to pizza peel or flat baking sheet.

4. Immediately spread with enough of the ricotta mixture to evenly coat dough. Sprinkle candied orange peel and chopped pistachios over the ricotta; shave additional chocolate over all. Dust with confectioner's sugar if desired, cut into squares and serve.

As you can probably guess, I did not leave that amazing little place until I had purchased a box full of cannoli and other tasty treats. What an amazing afternoon! And when Jen called to ask what I had been doing, I said proudly, "I went for a long walk."

Jonathan's Apple Crumb 'Pie'zza

My nephew Jonathan would walk across hot coals for one of my apple crumb pies. Well, maybe he wouldn't go that far, but I know that of all the things I cook and bake for family gatherings, my apple crumb pie is his absolute favorite. His question is never, 'Is Aunt Linda going to be here?'...it is always, 'Is Aunt Linda bringing her apple crumb pie?' Love you too, Jon.

8 to 9 ounces Dessert Pizza Dough at room temperature (page 25)

1 tablespoon orange zest, grated on a Microplane®

¼ cup granulated sugar

½ teaspoon ground cinnamon

¼ teaspoon freshly grated nutmeg

4 tablespoons unsalted butter, divided

1 large McIntosh apple, peeled, cored and sliced into ¼ inch thick slices

1 large Granny Smith apple, peeled, cored and sliced into ¼ inch thick slices

3 tablespoons brown sugar

1 tablespoon all-purpose flour

⅛ teaspoon kosher salt

pinch allspice

2 tablespoons walnut (or other nut) oil

4 ounces shredded, extra sharp white cheddar cheese (about 1 cup). See cook's note.

2 tablespoons toasted walnuts chopped – if desired

2 tablespoons confectioner's sugar for dusting

1. Knead orange zest into the dough and set aside.
2. Combine granulated sugar, cinnamon and nutmeg in a small bowl.
3. In a large skillet, melt 2 tablespoons of the butter over medium heat. When butter foams, add apples and sprinkle with two tablespoons of the sugar mixture from step 2. Stir to combine. Sauté apples, stirring occasionally for about 5 minutes or until they are soft, but still holding their shape. Remove from heat and set aside to cool slightly.
4. In a small bowl, combine brown sugar, flour, salt and allspice. Cut in remaining 2 tablespoons of cold butter with a pastry blender. Set aside for topping.
5. Roll, stretch and shape dough into an unrefined 12 to 14 inch circular or rectangular shape according to basic directions. Place on a rimless cookie sheet or pizza peel that has been lightly dusted with cornmeal. Brush dough with walnut oil and sprinkle with remaining 2 tablespoons sugar mixture from step 2.
6. Sprinkle shredded cheddar cheese over dough and arrange apples in a pleasing design over the cheese. Crumble reserved brown sugar/butter topping over all.
7. Bake on a preheated Pizza Grill or on a preheated pizza stone in a 500° F. oven, rotating after the first 4 minutes to prevent sticking. Bake for 10 to 12 minutes or until crust is firm and topping is melted and bubbling.
8. Remove from heat, garnish with chopped walnuts if desired and dust with confectioner's sugar. Allow 'pie'zza to rest for a few minutes, then cut and serve.

COOK'S NOTE: *Before baking, top pizza with shards of cheddar cheese to achieve a heightened cheddar flavor.*

Tip

To dust with sugar, place confectioner's sugar into a small strainer and tap strainer lightly as you pass it over the top of the pizza.

Mary's Marvelous Lemon Tart Pizza

My mother-in-law Mary was born and raised in Freeland, PA; my father-in-law Charles in Hazleton, PA. Their tastes in food were incredibly simplistic; they enjoyed food that I would consider plain. Charles loved scrapple, frozen peas that were defrosted and served cold in a small bowl of water and shoo fly pie. Mary never raved about any particular food which in and of itself was a foreign concept to me since most members of my family could ramble deliriously for days over Aunt Lena's linguini and clams or cousin Lucille's 'scharole' and beans. I guess you could say she ate to live, whereas we lived to eat!

I vividly remember the first time I had dinner at my soon to be in-laws' home; Mary made spaghetti, a dish I'm sure she chose knowing I was Italian and it was a safe bet that I would enjoy it. Well, let's just say I really appreciated the thought... the spaghetti was another story! After we were all seated, Mary placed a rather small serving bowl filled with a tomato soup colored sauce containing spaghetti that had been broken into pieces on the table. I immediately thought, 'That's good for me, I wonder what everyone else is going to eat.' You see, my mother made spaghetti two pounds at a time, and that was when she was serving it as a side dish! Mary's sauce was sweet and good, but not the rich, thick Sunday 'gravy' to which I was accustomed. My husband Charlie had an equally disconcerting experience eating with my family for the first time. He knew and enjoyed very basic cuisine, plain food accompanied by a salad with no dressing. It's no wonder he almost passed out when my mother placed a rather large serving (he was company) of salad dripping with oil and vinegar dressing onto his dinner plate; yes, the one that just a few seconds before had contained a huge piece of her home made lasagna. But, I digress. Mary also made her special dessert for me that evening...lemon tarts. I remember how she used to line them up in rows on cooling racks for a few hours before chilling them. Those little unadorned lemon tarts were quite marvelous even though she used pre-made frozen tart shells which she carefully 'baked' and lemon pudding and pie filling – from the box with love! My husband and his sister Barbara still name these tarts as their favorite dessert that their mother made. Mary and Charles are no longer with us, but to this day, I can still hear Charles after every company meal saying, "Well, mother, you've done it again!"

1 **(3 ounce) box lemon pudding and pie filling – Jell-O® Cook and Serve**

1 **cup mascarpone cheese**

½ **teaspoon vanilla extract**

3 **tablespoons granulated sugar**

8 to 9 ounces prepared Dessert Pizza Dough at room temperature (page 25)

1 **tablespoon candied lemon peel, chopped**

2 **tablespoons walnut oil (other nut oil or canola oil can be used)**

½ **pint fresh raspberries**

small fresh mint leaves for garnish

1 Prepare lemon pudding according to package directions; cool, stirring occasionally to prevent skin from forming on top of pudding. Place a piece of plastic wrap directly on pudding and chill thoroughly.

2 In a small bowl, combine mascarpone, vanilla and sugar. Stir until smooth; set aside.

3 Knead candied lemon peel into dough. Roll, stretch and shape dough into an unrefined rectangular shape approximately 12 by 14 inches according to basic directions. Brush both sides of the dough with walnut oil and place on a large rimless baking sheet or pizza peel that has been lightly dusted with cornmeal. Carefully lift dough and lay it on the pre-heated grill (see Grilled Pizza Primer.) Close grill lid and grill for 3 to 5 minutes or until bottom of crust is golden brown with darker grill marks. Turn over with tongs and grill for an additional 3 to 5 minutes until bottom is golden and crust is firm and golden. Remove from grill to pizza peel or flat baking sheet.

4 Immediately spread mascarpone mixture evenly over grilled dough. Spoon small dollops of lemon pudding randomly over cheese layer using about 1 to 1½ cups total.

5 Scatter raspberries around pizza and partially tuck small mint leaves under them for garnish.

6 Cut into squares and serve.

Tip

Look for candied lemon peel in specialty stores or online. You can substitute 1 tablespoon lemon zest tossed with 1 tablespoon granulated sugar for the candied lemon peel.

Nutty Nectarine Pizza

An amazing phenomenon in our family is that after indulging in one of our typical calorie laden meals, we could still look forward to dessert. Over the years, I found a unique way to justify having dessert – fruit! Whether we consumed an entire apple pie, a huge summer fruit tart with fresh whipped cream or bananas Foster with ice cream, we would all agree to go home and write "one fruit" in our diet diaries. This pizza is the ultimate fruit dessert. After moving to Arizona, it was only natural to include pistachios in my ultimate "fruit" dessert since these native nuts are naturally delicious. Feel free to substitute peaches for the nectarines and toasted almonds or walnuts for the pistachios. It still counts as one fruit!

4 tablespoons shelled pistachio nuts, 2 tablespoons finely chopped; 2 tablespoons coarsely chopped

8 to 9 ounces Dessert Pizza Dough at room temperature (page 25)

2 to 3 nectarines, ripe but firm; halved and pitted

3 tablespoons walnut oil, divided (substitute canola oil)

1 tablespoon granulated sugar

2 tablespoons brandy

1 cup mascarpone cheese at room temperature

½ teaspoon pure vanilla extract

1 Knead 2 tablespoons finely chopped pistachio nuts into dessert dough and set aside.

2 Brush nectarine halves with 1 tablespoon of the walnut oil. Grill over medium heat, cut side down, turning once or twice for about 5 minutes, or until grill marks appear and nectarines are heated through. Remove from heat and cut into ¼ inch thick slices. Place in a medium bowl, sprinkle with 1 tablespoons granulated sugar and drizzle with brandy. Toss to coat all slices, cover loosely with foil and set aside for about 10 minutes, stirring occasionally.

3 In a small bowl, combine mascarpone and vanilla; refrigerate until needed for topping.

4 Roll, stretch and shape dough into an unrefined rectangular shape approximately 12 by 14 inches according to basic directions. It may be easier to roll out this dough as the nuts may make it a bit more difficult to stretch. Brush both sides of the dough with walnut oil and place on a large rimless baking sheet or pizza peel that has been lightly dusted with cornmeal. Carefully lift dough and lay it on the preheated grill (see Grilled Pizza Primer.) Close grill lid and grill for 3 to 5 minutes or until bottom of crust is golden brown with darker grill marks. Turn over with tongs and grill for an additional 3 to 5 minutes until bottom is golden and crust is firm. Remove from grill to pizza peel or flat baking sheet; allow crust to cool for 1 to 2 minutes.

5 Spread cheese mixture in an even layer over grilled dough. Arrange drained nectarine slices neatly over cheese; top with the 2 tablespoons of coarsely chopped pistachio nuts.

6 Cut into small squares or wedges and serve immediately.

Sassy Sauces and Tasty Toppings

Just as clothes make the man, sauce can make your pizza - so sauce it wisely. Choose the best quality ingredients you can afford when making your sauces, knowing that a sauce will only be as good as each of its components; and a superior sauce will add incomparable complexity of flavor to your pizza.

In addition to a variety of tomato based sauces and unctuous cheese sauces, *Sassy Sauces and Tasty Toppings* includes a collection of recipes for pungent pesto, tapenade, caramelized onions, and garlic paste, among others which all serve equally well as pizza sauce. If it's edible and spreadable, you can sauce your pizza with it.

Peruse the *Sassy Sauces and Tasty Toppings* recipe index to find page references for a wide variety of pizza toppings recipes. Utilize any or all the recipes in this section regularly to make a favorite pizza or as go-to favorites for easy family lunches or dinners.

Many of the recipes in this chapter can be made in advance and frozen, or kept in the refrigerator for several days; thus, allowing you to pull together a remarkable pizza on remarkably short notice.

Marion's Marinara Sauce

My mother, Marion, was an amazing 'Italian' cook. Being of Czech and Russian descent, her Italian food repertoire was non-existent when she married my father, who was Italian to the core. Mom learned early on from her sisters-in-law and father-in-law, Grandpa Sorrentino, everything she needed to know in order to make Daddy's favorite foods—basically, anything Italian. Mom rarely used recipes and usually cooked large quantities of whatever she was making. Her tomato sauce had a taste all its own and her 'recipe' has evaded replication over the years. I think this sauce comes closest to the perfectly balanced taste I remember from years past. Thanks, Mom.

2 (28 ounce) cans San Marzano Italian plum tomatoes with basil

¼ cup extra virgin olive oil

2 ounces salt pork, cut into two or three strips

1 small yellow onion (approximately ¾ cup chopped)

3 cloves garlic, peeled

¼ cup parsley leaves (approximately 5 sprigs)

1 teaspoon kosher salt

½ teaspoon freshly ground pepper

¼ teaspoon dried oregano leaves or 2 small sprigs fresh oregano

6 fresh basil leaves torn

1 Place tomatoes into a large bowl. Crush tomatoes with your hands, removing any hard or light colored pieces of core. You may need to tuck a mopeen into your shirt, this could get messy!

2 Heat olive oil in a large saucepan over medium-low heat. Add salt pork to the pan and sauté 7 to 10 minutes or until all its fat is rendered. Add onion to pan and sauté 3 minutes, or until translucent.

3 Chop garlic and parsley together and add to pan along with salt and pepper. Stir to combine and sauté 1 to 2 minutes. Be careful not to allow the garlic to burn as it will turn bitter. If this happens, discard oil and onion mixture and begin again at step 2.

4 Stir in oregano and reserved tomatoes with their juice. Raise heat to high and bring to a boil. Reduce heat until sauce is at a very slow simmer and cook uncovered, stirring occasionally, for about 1 hour or until sauce is thickened to your liking.

5 If you used fresh oregano, remove sprigs. Remove salt pork and discard...or the kids may spit it out at the table like we immediately did after biting into one of the small diced pieces of plumped up fat that my mother left in the sauce. Stir in torn basil leaves if desired and cook 1 to 2 minutes longer. Remove from heat. You may use plum tomatoes without added basil for this recipe. If you do, you must add fresh basil in step 5; otherwise it is optional.

Sauce keeps in the refrigerator up to 3 days or you can freeze it for up to 3 months.

Sauce All' Amatriciana

Originally, sauce all' Amatriciana was made with cured pork from the inside of a pig's cheek (guanciale,) but in the absence of a pig willing to give up part of his cheek, you can use bacon, Canadian bacon or pancetta in its place.

3 tablespoons extra virgin olive oil

3 tablespoons unsalted butter

1 small yellow onion, finely chopped (4 to 6 ounces)

4 ounces good quality smoked bacon, pancetta or Canadian bacon, fine dice

3 cloves garlic, minced

½ teaspoon crushed red pepper, more or less to taste

1 (28 ounce) can San Marzano tomatoes, crushed by hand

½ teaspoon kosher salt, or to taste

freshly ground black pepper to taste

½ cup red wine

1 Heat oil in a medium sauté pan over medium heat, add butter and heat until butter foams. Add onion and sauté until transparent, about 5 minutes.

2 Add bacon and sauté until crisp and most of fat is rendered, 7 to 10 minutes. Stir in garlic and cook for 30 seconds.

3 Add crushed red pepper, tomatoes, salt and freshly ground black pepper to taste. Stir in red wine and cook uncovered over medium low heat at a steady simmer, stirring occasionally for 45 to 50 minutes or until slightly thickened. Fat should be slightly separated from tomatoes at this point.

Yield – 3 cups

Tip

To hand crush tomatoes, place them in a good size bowl and crush carefully (or wear a mopeen) removing any hard pieces of cores that remain.

Sofrito
Basic Spanish Tomato Sauce

Sofrito is a simple, versatile Spanish puree-like tomato sauce that adds an amazing depth of flavor to a variety of traditional Spanish dishes. You can experiment with different types of peppers and seasonings to come up with your own version of this traditional Spanish sauce. Have fun!

1 can whole, peeled tomatoes (28 ounces)

¼ cup Spanish olive oil

1 large Spanish onion, finely chopped (8 ounces)

1 red bell pepper, cored, seeded and cut into ¼ inch dice

1 Anaheim pepper, cored, seeded and cut into ¼ inch dice

4 cloves garlic, minced

1 teaspoon Spanish sweet paprika

1 teaspoon kosher salt, or to taste

freshly ground black pepper to taste

1 Place tomatoes and their juice into a large bowl. Crush tomatoes with your hands, removing any hard or light colored pieces of core; set aside.

2 Heat olive oil in a medium sauté pan over medium to medium-low heat. Add onions and cook for 10 minutes or until onion is translucent and just beginning to brown.

3 Add red bell and Anaheim peppers and sauté, stirring often for 10 minutes; add garlic, stir and cook for 1 minute.

4 Add tomatoes and paprika; stir to combine. Raise heat and bring mixture to a boil. Lower heat and simmer uncovered, stirring often, for 20 to 30 minutes or until mixture is thickened. Add salt and freshly ground black pepper to taste.

5 Cool before using on your pizza. You can refrigerate this sauce, covered for up to one week or freeze for up to 2 months.

Yield – 3½ cups

Dijon Béchamel Sauce

Dijon mustard gives this basic béchamel sauce a boost, transforming it into the perfect complement for dishes featuring the saltiness of ham and the sweetness of pineapple.

- **2 cups whole milk**
- **4 tablespoons unsalted butter**
- **4 tablespoons all-purpose flour**
- **¾ teaspoon kosher salt**
- **¼ teaspoon freshly ground black pepper**
- **pinch freshly grated nutmeg**
- **2 tablespoons Dijon mustard**

1. Scald milk in a small saucepan; set aside.
2. Melt butter in a medium saucepan over medium heat. Stir in flour; cook, stirring continuously until completely blended, about 2 minutes. Do not allow flour to brown.
3. Add one half of the hot milk to flour mixture, whisking to combine. Add remaining milk and whisk until smooth. Add salt and pepper; cook at a slow bubble, stirring constantly until thickened. Stir in Dijon mustard and nutmeg. Remove from heat and set aside to cool slightly.

HELPFUL HINT: *This sauce will keep in the refrigerator for up to two days. Place a piece of plastic wrap directly on the surface and cover container tightly. Reheat sauce in the top of a double boiler.*

Yield – 2 cups

Provolone Cheese Sauce

Add piquant provolone cheese to basic béchamel sauce and you have created the most wonderful cheese sauce imaginable. This sauce can be used as a base for many pizzas, especially ones topped with prosciutto. However, my favorite way to use this sauce is to stir in some cooked lobster meat, mix with al dente cavatappi pasta and bake the combination on my favorite pizza dough. It is truly out of this world.

- **2 cups whole milk**
- **1 cup heavy cream**
- **4 tablespoons unsalted butter**
- **¼ cup all-purpose flour**
- **1 teaspoon kosher salt**
- **¼ teaspoon freshly ground black pepper**
- **1 cup shredded, imported provolone cheese**
- **¼ cup freshly grated Parmigiano-Reggiano cheese**
- **¼ teaspoon freshly grated nutmeg**

1 Scald milk in a small saucepan; set aside

2 Melt butter in a medium saucepan over medium heat. Stir in flour; cook, stirring continuously until completely blended, about 2 minutes. Do not allow flour to brown.

3 Add one half of the hot milk/cream to flour mixture, whisking to combine. Add remaining milk/cream and whisk until smooth. Add salt and pepper; cook at a slow bubble, stirring constantly until thickened. Remove from heat and stir in provolone cheese, Parmigiano, and nutmeg. Stir until cheese has melted.

Yield – 3 cups

Classic Caramelized Onions

1¼ pounds large yellow or sweet onions such as Vidalia, thinly sliced and separated into rings

2 tablespoons extra virgin olive oil

2 tablespoons unsalted butter

½ teaspoon kosher salt

1 tablespoon granulated sugar

1 Heat oil in a wide sauté pan over medium heat.

2 Add butter and heat until butter foams. Once foam subsides, add onions and stir in salt. Cover pan and sauté over low heat for 20 minutes, shaking pan occasionally to mix.

3 Remove cover, sprinkle with sugar and stir to combine. Sauté for 30 to 40 minutes longer, stirring occasionally. Be careful not to let the onions burn – this can happen very quickly. Slow and low cooking is the key to achieving perfect caramelizing.

4 Sauté until onions are a deep golden brown color.

Yield - Approximately 1 cup – or enough for one pizza

Bacon Caramelized Onions

Use this recipe in place of the Classic Caramelized Onions when you want a more savory onion base for your pizza.

4 ounces bacon (approximately 5-6 slices), cut into ½ inch pieces

1¼ pounds yellow onions, thinly sliced and somewhat separated into rings

1 teaspoon fresh thyme leaves, chopped or ½ teaspoon dry thyme leaves

1 Heat a large sauté pan over medium-high heat. When pan is hot, add bacon and cook, stirring to separate the pieces until all the fat has been rendered, about 7 minutes. Remove with a slotted spoon. Drain on a paper towel lined plate and reserve for use of your choice. If using for pizza topping, remove from fat as soon as pieces are lightly browned.

2 Add onions and thyme to the bacon drippings; stir and lower heat to medium low. Cook, tossing occasionally with tongs, for 50 to 60 minutes, or until completely softened and golden brown in color. It is very important not to rush this process as it is about caramelizing and not just about browning the onions.

Yield – Approximately 1 cup

Tip

This will keep in the refrigerator up to three days. To freeze, cool caramelized onions and seal in a 2½ cup plastic container. Once frozen, remove from plastic container and seal in a one quart zip top freezer bag. Thaw completely and bring to room temperature before using on your pizza.

Roasted Garlic Paste (oven or grill method)

- **4 heads garlic**
- **4 tablespoons extra virgin olive oil**
- **½ teaspoon kosher salt**
- **¼ teaspoon freshly ground black pepper**
- **1 tablespoon fresh thyme leaves, chopped**

1. Preheat oven to 375° F.
2. Peel away any loose layers of outer skin from garlic heads.
3. Slice off top ¼ inch from each head, being sure to expose a bit of each clove. Place close together cut side up on a square of heavy duty aluminum foil. Pour oil over garlic heads. Sprinkle with salt, pepper and thyme.
4. Crimp foil into an airtight pouch and bake for approximately one hour or until cloves are soft and skins are beginning to split.
5. Unseal top of foil to expose heads of garlic and bake until golden brown, 10 to 15 minutes longer.
6. Allow to cool slightly. Remove cloves from skins by squeezing gently from bottom of head. Place in a small bowl and mash with a fork. Add a drizzle of the oil in which the garlic roasted and stir until smooth.

Tip

This paste will keep for up to two days tightly covered in the refrigerator or for several months in the freezer.

TO PREPARE USING GAS GRILL METHOD

1. Heat grill to medium high.
2. After completing steps 2 and 3 from the oven method above, wrap garlic heads loosely with foil and place on grill over indirect heat. Grill for about 1 hour, or until cloves are soft and golden brown.

Yield – Approximately ½ cup or enough for one or two pizzas depending on intensity of garlic flavor desired.

Slow Roasted Tomatoes

- **2 to 3 pounds plum or Roma tomatoes (12 tomatoes)**
- **¼ cup extra virgin olive oil**
- **1 large head garlic, cloves separated, peeled and left whole**
- **1 teaspoon kosher salt**
- **½ teaspoon freshly ground black pepper**

1. Preheat oven to 250° F.
2. Halve tomatoes lengthwise, lightly squeeze to remove seeds and leave cores intact.
3. Place tomatoes close together; cut side up on a sheet pan. Scatter garlic cloves among tomatoes. Drizzle with olive oil; sprinkle with salt and pepper. Turn each tomato half over so cut side is down on sheet pan. Brush outside of tomato with a bit more olive oil.
4. Roast for 2 to 3 hours, turning tomatoes over after 1 hour. Open the oven door periodically for a second or two allowing steam to escape. Bake until tomatoes are shriveled, but still slightly juicy in the center. This may take as long as 4 hours, but it is so worth the wait.
5. If not using immediately, cool and place into a container. Cover with the oil from the roasting pan. Refrigerate for one week or freeze.

Yield - 24 halves

Italian Meatballs

Just like Momma used to make!

- **1 pound ground beef**
- **¼ cup dried bread crumbs**
- **¼ cup Parmigiano-Reggiano cheese, grated**
- **¼ cup fresh flat Italian parsley leaves**
- **2 cloves garlic**
- **½ teaspoon kosher salt**
- **½ teaspoon freshly ground black pepper**
- **1 egg, slightly beaten with 1 tablespoon milk**

1. Preheat oven to 400° F.
2. Mince garlic and parsley together.
3. Combine all ingredients in a medium mixing bowl and lightly mix with a fork or your hands.
4. Divide mixture into 6 equal parts. Shape mixture into balls, having a bit of olive oil on your hands to coat meatballs.
5. Bake in a shallow, lightly oiled baking pan for 20 minutes or until lightly browned.

COOK'S NOTE: *Meatballs can be prepared up to 2 months in advance. After shaping meatballs, place on a flat tray and freeze them for about two hours. Remove from tray and place in a zip-top freezer bag or other airtight container. When ready to use, defrost meatballs overnight in the refrigerator and bake as in step 5 above.*

Momma's Meatloaf

This meatloaf has been a hit with my family for years. However, in the old days, I didn't measure anything...it took too long! After making this recipe a few times, you may choose to adjust seasonings to your taste. This pairs well with garlic mashed potatoes and peas – my 'go to' comfort food meal for cold winter nights in Connecticut.

- **2 pounds ground beef (a mixture of 90% and 80% lean)**
- **¼ cup onion, finely chopped**
- **1 clove garlic, minced**
- **1 teaspoon kosher salt**
- **½ teaspoon freshly ground black pepper**
- **2 eggs, slightly beaten**
- **½ cup dry bread crumbs, unseasoned**
- **½ cup whole milk**
- **2 tablespoons BBQ sauce, plus additional for topping**
- **1 teaspoon Worcestershire® sauce**
- **1 teaspoon fresh thyme leaves, chopped**
- **¼ cup fresh flat parsley leaves, chopped**

1. Preheat oven to 375° F.
2. Place ground beef in a large bowl and lightly separate with a large fork.
3. Add remaining ingredients, evenly distributing them over entire surface of beef to facilitate incorporation.
4. Lightly, but thoroughly mix all ingredients into beef with a large fork or your hands. It is important not to over mix as your meatloaf will be dense and tough.
5. Lightly oil a medium size baking pan with low sides; bring meat mixture together in the bowl and place onto the baking pan. Shape into a loaf and drizzle additional BBQ sauce over top if desired. Bake for about 1 hour and 15 minutes, or until internal temperature reaches 160° F.
6. Allow to rest for about 10 minutes before slicing.

Basil Pesto

When preparing this pesto, choose basil leaves that are small and fresh; do not include any stems in your pesto as this can result in a bitter taste.

- **2 cups fresh basil leaves, washed and dried**
- **2 to 3 cloves garlic, peeled and roughly chopped**
- **¼ cup pine nuts**
- **½ teaspoon kosher salt**
- **½ teaspoon freshly ground black pepper**
- **½ cup Parmigiano-Reggiano cheese, freshly grated**
- **3 to 4 ounces extra virgin olive oil**

1. Combine basil leaves, pine nuts and garlic in a food processor. Pulse three or four times to puree; add salt and pepper, pulsing to combine.
2. With the motor running, add oil in a steady stream through feed tube into basil mixture and process until combined. Add more or less oil as needed to achieve desired consistency - smooth and fluid - not too loose or too thick.
3. Add Parmigiano cheese and pulse several times to combine.

HELPFUL HINT: *Extra pesto can be stored for several days in the refrigerator or frozen for future use. To store in refrigerator, place pesto into a small container and float enough olive oil over top to completely seal pesto underneath. Cover tightly.*

Yield - 1 cup

Cilantro Pesto

- **2 cups cilantro leaves - about 2 bunches, leaves removed from stems**
- **2 cloves garlic, roughly chopped**
- **¼ cup Toasted Pine Nuts (page 18)**
- **½ teaspoon kosher salt**
- **½ teaspoon freshly ground black pepper**
- **3 ounces extra virgin olive oil**
- **¼ cup Cotija or Parmigiano-Regiano cheese, freshly grated**

1. Combine cilantro leaves, garlic, and pine nuts in a food processor. Pulse three or four times to puree; add salt and pepper, pulsing to combine.
2. With the motor running, add oil in a steady stream through feed tube into cilantro mixture, processing until combined. Add more or less oil as needed to achieve desired consistency - smooth and fluid - not too loose or too thick.
3. Stir in Cotija or Parmigiano cheese and pulse to combine.

Yield - 1 cup

Roasted Red Pepper Pesto

- **3 large red bell peppers**
- **½ cup fresh basil leaves, torn**
- **¼ cup pine nuts, toasted**
- **3 large cloves garlic, peeled and roughly chopped**
- **½ teaspoon kosher salt, plus more for finishing**
- **½ teaspoon freshly ground black pepper, plus more for finishing**
- **2 to 3 ounces extra virgin olive oil**
- **½ cup Parmigiano-Reggiano cheese, freshly grated on a Microplane®**
- **½ teaspoon balsamic vinegar**

Tip

Extra pesto can be stored in a tightly covered container for several days in the refrigerator.

1 Preheat a grill or broiler to high. Place whole peppers on grate of grill or on a broiler pan so peppers are 2 inches from element. Blacken peppers for about 10 to 15 minutes, turning often. Once skins are almost completely blackened and blistered, remove peppers from heat. Place peppers into a brown paper bag on a plate and fold top of bag to seal or place peppers in a bowl and seal with plastic wrap for about 10 minutes or until peppers have had a chance to sweat and soften a bit more. Remove from bag or bowl and peel off skin with your fingers...messy, but worth the effort! Do not be tempted to do this under running water as you will wash away much of the wonderful flavor. Cut off top and base of each pepper and slice it open. Scrape off membranes and seeds with a knife. Cut into strips. Once cooled, place peppers, basil leaves, toasted pine nuts and garlic into a food processor fitted with a metal blade. Pulse 3 or 4 times to puree; add salt and pepper, pulsing to combine.

2 With motor running, add oil in a steady stream through feed tube into pepper mixture until combined. Add more or less oil as needed to achieve desired consistency – smooth and fluid – not too loose or too thick.

3 With motor off, add Parmigiano-Reggiano cheese and balsamic vinegar, then pulse to combine. Taste pesto then add salt and pepper to adjust seasoning as desired.

Yield – 2 cups

Mushroom Tapenade

- **1 tablespoon extra virgin olive oil**
- **2 tablespoons unsalted butter**
- **2 tablespoons shallots, finely chopped**
- **1 clove garlic, minced**
- **1 pound mushrooms, cleaned and chopped - I use half button mushrooms and half crimini mushrooms**
- **½ teaspoon kosher salt**
- **⅛ teaspoon freshly ground pepper**
- **2 teaspoons fresh thyme leaves, finely chopped**

1 Heat a large sauté pan over medium heat. Place oil and butter into the pan and heat until butter foams. Add shallots and cook for 1 to 2 minutes or until slightly softened and translucent. Add garlic and cook for 30 seconds.

2 Add chopped mushrooms, salt, and pepper. Stir and raise heat to medium high. Cook, stirring often until all juice from the mushrooms evaporates, about 7 to 10 minutes. Add thyme and stir for 30 seconds to 1 minute until thoroughly combined.

3 Remove from heat, cool. This can be made a day ahead and stored in the refrigerator. Bring to room temperature before using.

Yield - 1½ cups

Sassy Sauces and Tasty Toppings ~ Recipe Index

Measurements Equivalent Chart

CUP	FLUID OUNCE	TABLESPOON	TEASPOON
1/16 cup	.5 ounce	1 tablespoon	3 teaspoons
1/8 cup	1 ounce	2 tablespoons	6 teaspoons
1/4 cup	2 ounces	4 tablespoons	12 teaspoons
1/3 cup	3 ounces	5 tablespoons +1 teaspoon	16 teaspoons
1/2 cup	4 ounces	8 tablespoons	24 teaspoons
2/3 cup	5 ounces	1 tablespoons +2 teaspoons	32 teaspoons
3/4 cup	6 ounces	12 tablespoons	36 teaspoons
1 cup	8 ounces	16 tablespoons	48 teaspoons

Index

E

F

G

H

J

K

L

T

W

Z

Notes